THE PRESIDENTIAL PARDON

The
PRESIDENTIAL PARDON

The SHORT CLAUSE
with a LONG,
TROUBLED HISTORY

Saikrishna Bangalore Prakash

HARVARD UNIVERSITY PRESS
Cambridge, Massachusetts • London, England
2026

Publication of this book has been supported through
the generous provisions of the
Maurice and Lula Bradley Smith Memorial Fund

EU GPSR Authorized Representative
LOGOS Europe, 9 rue Nicolas Poussin, 17000,
La Rochelle, France
E-mail: contact@logoseurope.eu

Library of Congress Cataloging-in-Publication Data

Names: Prakash, Saikrishna Bangalore author
Title: The presidential pardon : the short clause with a long,
troubled history / Saikrishna Bangalore Prakash.
Description: Cambridge, Massachusetts : Harvard University Press, 2026. |
Includes bibliographical references and index.
Identifiers: LCCN 2025032460 (print) | LCCN 2025032461 (ebook) |
ISBN 9780674303201 cloth | ISBN 9780674303881 epub | ISBN 9780674303898 pdf
Subjects: LCSH: Pardon—United States | Presidents—United States |
Executive power—United States | LCGFT: Law materials
Classification: LCC KF9695 .P73 2026 (print) | LCC KF9695 (ebook) |
DDC 345.73/077—dc23/eng/20250904
LC record available at https://lccn.loc.gov/2025032460
LC ebook record available at https://lccn.loc.gov/2025032461

To Gayathri, Gauri, and Aditi Lakshmi,
You are like daughters to me,
My Chinna, Chimpu, and Shamitha

Contents

Twenty Words

IN THE NOT-SO-DISTANT PAST, a collection of wise men assembled to form a more perfect union. Among other things, they sought to establish *justice*. They launched three vital branches— legislative, executive, and judicial—each tasked to wield the powers traditionally associated with such institutions. While the legislative and judicial authority was dispersed across many hands, executive authority was concentrated in a "president."

Amid the passages creating and describing the executive was a terse clause, just twenty words long, tacked onto the end of a list of powers, almost as an afterthought: *he shall have Power to grant Reprieves and Pardons for Offences against the United States, except in Cases of Impeachment.*[1] This seemingly innocuous clause was pregnant with vast and incredible powers. One man (and today, one person), wielding a pen, could waive all sorts of fines, forfeitures, and penalties, unshackle scores of prisoners, and overrule death sentences. As noteworthy as these illustrations are, they only scratch the surface of the array of clemency options at his fingertips. What one famous jurist said of the British Crown may be equally said of our president: our first magistrate may "soften the rigour of the general law, in such criminal cases as merit an exemption from punishment."[2] This authority is undeniably potent and astounding.

In *The Merchant of Venice*, Portia declares that "The quality of mercy is not strain'd, It droppeth as the gentle rain from heaven / Upon the place beneath: it is twice blest; It blesseth him that gives and him that takes."[3] Indeed, clemency for me in no way precludes leniency for you. Further, some might imagine that mercy is a blessing for all.

Yet despite what Portia says, pardons can sometimes seem a curse, as when the wicked or unrepentant receive forgiveness. Precisely because mercy is not an unalloyed good, some opposed the Pardon Clause. They beheld a malignancy, not a blessing, dreading that it vested too much authority in one man. The president might wield the pardon pen to advance his personal interests and conceal his machinations. Even the most ardent supporters of the proposed framework could not wholly dismiss these concerns. Despite such anxieties, the Constitution was ratified and made into supreme law.

In the earliest years, such fears must have seemed hyperbolic. The first man to hold the first chair was the epitome of a faithful executive, perhaps the most steadfast and selfless we have ever had. From the first president's pardon pen, deftly and judiciously employed, came mercy for ordinary criminals and reconciliation with (tax) rebels. His unblemished clemency record appeared to refute the critics of the Constitution's Pardon Clause, the ones who foresaw perversions and travesties and generally prophesied that pardons would be instruments of base politics. None of that happened while George Washington helmed the government.

Yet if entropy is an iron law of physics, then corruption is an iron law of politics. All political institutions tend toward corruption, with awesome powers given for noble purposes perverted to promote the narrow interests of officials. If men were angels, there would be no need for government.[4] But men are not angels, neither the governed nor the governors. It was inevitable that cynical observers would perceive particular pardons as corrupt, concluding that an instrument of mercy had been wrongly exploited. Even worse, the perception often resembled reality, as some pardons did advance the partisan, policy, and personal interests of our presidents.

Shortly after the father of our country departed the presidency, the righteous fable of a pardon power above politics was fractured irretrievably. Starting with John Adams and Thomas Jefferson, through Abraham Lincoln and Andrew Johnson, through Gerald Ford, George H. W. Bush, and Bill Clinton, there have been four troubling threads. Presidents issued pardons to further their political or personal interests; they showered clemency on partisan allies; their pardons undermined justice; and some members of the public perceived them as issuing unseemly pardons, ones that sapped confidence in the rule of law. Not all (or even most) pardons evoked these concerns or raised these perceptions. But the awful ones could appear truly appalling, and they sometimes eclipsed the salutary ones. While Lady Justice wears a blindfold as she holds aloft her scales of justice, neither presidents nor the American people are blind. Our presidents always dispense pardons with their eyes wide open, granting clemency that too often raises legitimate suspicions. When ordinary Americans see such pardons, we behold scales of justice that seem uneven, even broken. When it comes to pardons, We the People are gripped by skepticism, even dark suspicions.

Over the last decade or so, the cynicism has metastasized. Joseph Biden ran on a campaign of nullifying marijuana laws and, once in office, he redeemed his pledge, using the pardon pen not once, but twice.[5] These amnesties may seem like small potatoes because many Americans oppose marijuana prohibition and hence there was never going to be an uproar.[6] Nonetheless, they raised a profound question: Should a president pledged to faithfully execute the law be able to undo entire laws with a stroke (or two) of the pen? Biden's amnesties approached a suspension of the law, and one must wonder what other quasi-suspensions of the law are on the horizon. Are tax or environmental penalties next?

The real ire and indignation would erupt at the end of his term. Biden had spent much of his political life allowing his family to sell access to him; he was not going to depart the Oval Office leaving them cowering under a Damocles Sword, subject to expensive and frightening prosecutions.[7] He granted his son a remarkable pardon covering *all* federal offenses committed over *ten years*. It covered not only tax and gun possession violations, but also whatever else he might have done, no matter how shocking.[8] The clemency for Biden's siblings and in-laws also extended for more than ten years, except that their pardon covered only nonviolent offenses.[9] Finally, Biden pardoned political allies, some of whom might have faced prosecution. He cited the potential for prosecutorial abuse by a successor (Donald Trump) bent on retribution.[10] Biden's fierce opponents regarded the last set of pardons as immunizing those who had persecuted or thwarted President Donald Trump; these critics regarded these pardons as partisan, ones designed to thwart justice.[11] In the years and decades to come, would every president leaving the Oval Office issue a flurry of pardons to allies? A rabid, partisan official who expected a pardon at the end of a president's term might be steeled to purpose, pursuing enemies and presidential agendas with extra zeal, knowing that forgiveness would come soon.

As awful as Biden's pardons appeared, Donald Trump would do his best to match and exceed Biden. Bracketing the Biden Interregnum were "Trump 45" and "Trump 47." During Trump 45, the pardon pen became an instrument of securing favorable press and winning news cycles. Bypassing career pardon officials and their cautious recommendations, the president concentrated power in the White House and made decisions designed to win plaudits from celebrities and influencers.[12] It was a pardon reality show, starring the former host of *The Apprentice*. Instead of declaring "You're fired," the president declared, "You're pardoned!" It was often must-see TV, with celebrities like Kim Kardashian and Deion Sanders in the mix. Some luminaries sought pardons for others, acting altruistically or seeking to burnish their own images.[13] Other stars received clemency, ensuring that media outlets would proclaim the good news and report the reactions of their many fans.[14] Although there was talk of pardoning the January 6 rioters and a possible self-pardon, none of that came to pass. The worst seemed averted. Pardon policy might have descended into tawdry theater, but it was not an utter disaster.

Four years later, in Trump 47, the president was back to pardoning to win headlines. But like his predecessor, President Trump had also campaigned on clemency, and followed through on his promise; his pardon of violent January 6ers dismayed many Republicans, not to mention many other Americans.[15] Further, there was the ongoing, sordid business of lobbyists charging millions to ensure that a pardon petition received the president's attention.[16] Finally, the president has rewarded campaign contributors with pardons, raising the specter of cash-for-clemency.[17] It seems that the quality of mercy *is* strained, mainly restricted to the wealthy and the connected. Again, justice is not blind to influence, wealth, contributions, and electoral calculations, at least where the president is concerned. It all looks awful. It feels awful. It is awful.

We find ourselves in a brave new world, where presidents already drunk on unilateralism—lawbreaking, lawmaking, and warmaking—are belatedly embracing the full and astounding potential of the pardon pen. Candidates can promise pardons to their voters and allies ("I will pardon you and your loved ones"). Once in office, presidents can neuter laws that they (and their coalition) detest—relating to, say, marijuana, tax, or immigration. They can immunize their lawbreaking friends and allies. And sometimes, even when a president is not seeking any sort of advantage, the public and the incumbent's opponents will perceive them as pursuing personal or partisan ends. Much as Carl von Clausewitz said of war, pardons have become the continuation of politics by other means.[18] As presidents wield the pardon pen, they advance their ideological and personal agendas, bolster their electoral bases, inflict psychic wounds on opponents, and wreak havoc upon the rule of law.

From the point of view of modern presidents, the power of the pardon is uniquely attractive. The Constitution famously establishes checks and balances. The president cannot make treaties, for example, without the Senate's consent.[19] The president ordinarily cannot appoint to high offices without the Senate's approval.[20] The president is checked by the courts, as when they order the executive to take an action or to halt some initiative. The president can propose, but cannot make, laws.[21]

The presidential pardon power is distinct. Checks and balances do not apply. The Constitution does not impose many limits, and, according to established judicial doctrine, Congress cannot impose any additional ones. And whereas in prior ages one's sense of shame functioned as a check, that sentiment now seems in short supply, while cheek is in abundance. Presidents seem unabashed, basking in the inevitable approval of their cronies and confident that their allies will stoutly defend them from the negative nabobs and tut-tutters.

This book introduces Americans to their Pardon Clause, a regal remnant that, in some respects, renders the president more powerful than the British monarch of the eighteenth century. It will discuss the hopes and fears surrounding the clause, the political controversies it has stirred up, and what the pardon power has become. Chapter 1 discusses the creation of the clause and the fears it triggered. Chapter 2 introduces some pardon basics, dissecting the clause. Chapter 3 discusses George Washington's grants of clemency, arguing that he approached the system with the proper care and disinterest. Chapter 4 recounts several infamous pardon controversies, each of which involved a claim that the president was advancing political interests in exercising the pardon pen. Chapter 5 takes up the midnight pardons of Joseph Biden and the inauguration amnesty of Donald Trump. Chapter 6 argues that we are amidst a pardon dystopia, where the pardon power is seen mostly (or merely) as an instrument of partisan politics and personal advancement. If almost every other area of government has become corrupted in some way, and if the Biden and Trump pardons represent a type of corruption, then we can expect the pardon pen to be seen as yet another tool mired in the muck of politics. Chapter 7 discusses reforms.

While I will make a few remarks about mercy, rehabilitation, and calibration, I will not discuss the role of clemency in penal reform or ethical perspectives on pardons, justice, and mercy. Rather, this text will reflect my expertise in the separation of powers and my judgment, previously expressed in *The Living Presidency,* that the modern president has become a progressively faithless executive, sacrificing the rule of law in pursuit of the incumbent's interests.[22] Consistent with that view, I sense that the pardon pen is no longer much of an instrument of justice or mercy, but increasingly a weapon of partisan politics and personal aggrandizement. It retains the trappings of and a vestigial link to mercy and justice, but the connection is wearing thin.

Nor will this book analyze the considerable good that flows (or might flow) from the pardon pen. There are, of course, many just things that presidents can do with that pen. Of the thousands of pardons our presidents have issued, many (most?) were in service of mercy, justice, and making the punishment better fit the crime. A comprehensive evaluation of US pardon policy would require considering all past acts of clemency, and then evaluating (and second-guessing) them in light of multifarious factors: the crime, the sentence, retribution, deterrence, calibration, equal treatment, mercy, and more. This is an impossible task. I will say, however, that considerable good also could arise from a *different* pardon regime. Perhaps we can reform the pardon power in a way that generates far less heat and far more acclaim.

From the perspective of modern executives seeking to maximize their authority, popularity, and reelection chances, the pardon pen is delightfully unilateral, uniquely powerful, extraordinarily easy to wield, and utterly final. No need to navigate a slothful, obstructionist, and poisonous Congress; no need to persuade some egg-headed judge. Reward friends by doling out pardons like candy. Demoralize enemies by shielding or liberating their foes. Act with absolute impunity, for no one can prosecute presidents for their pardons, and no president is likely to be ousted from office. Of course, the pardon pen cannot gratify all the president's policy and personal impulses. Nonetheless, the number of things that the president can do with that instrument is surprising. Its usage will only bloom and grow, as other branches watch and groan.

It is hard to overstate the power of the pardon pen. Consider an analogy. Monopoly, the board game by Hasbro, has two "Get out of jail free" cards, one from the "Community Chest" pile and one from the "Chance" stack. These cards are valuable because they enable a person to avoid jail, a purgatory where their play essentially stops for a spell. Indeed, the cards are so valuable that they can be sold to other players. Well, our president can issue "Get out of jail free cards" too. Except these are *genuine* get out of jail free cards. Further, our Pardoner-in-Chief can issue hundreds, thousands, maybe millions of them.

Tomorrow, next year, or in the coming decade, a president could, if she chose, liberate all federal prisoners and pardon all federal offenders, including those yet to be apprehended or prosecuted. This might seem a fantasy, but remember: some politicians oppose overcriminalization and others wish to abolish the police. In that context, it is easy to imagine a candidate running on a promise of sweeping clemency because she supposes punishments are too draconian or otherwise unjust. Imagine a chief executive who believed that some federal punishments, say for theft and hard drug use, were too severe. With a general commutation, that president could convert Congress's mandatory minimum sentences into mere recommendations. Death sentences could drop to a decade in jail.

Ten-year sentences could become ten days. With an active pardon pen, presidents can effectively rewrite some of our laws, no matter what Congress thinks.

We must either make our peace with our clemency dystopia or push for pardon reform, perhaps even constitutional amendments. If our presidents have shifted from faithful law enforcers to political creatures moved by personal or partisan motives, we must reconsider and reform how America dispenses mercy.

THE PRESIDENTIAL PARDON

CHAPTER I

An Eighteenth-Century Clause

BARABBAS is the most famous recipient of a pardon, at least in the Western world. Barabbas was a murderer, thief, and insurrectionist, or so it is said. Pilate, the Roman governor of Judea, offered an assembled crowd the choice between liberating Jesus of Nazareth or Jesus Barabbas (Jesus was a common name).[1] Some scholars assert that it was Passover and that the Jews customarily pardoned on festive occasions.[2] The Jews were not unique, for history has witnessed many "festive pardons." In any event, the throng selected Barabbas, and Pilate immediately released him. Jesus received no clemency, and the Romans crucified him. Jesus is the most celebrated person *not* to receive a pardon.

Pardons existed elsewhere in the Middle East, as the Quran attests. Muhammad pardoned those who had insulted or opposed him, particularly after they converted. With submission (Islam) came forgiveness.[3]

According to the Mahabharata, the great sage Kashyapa once said, "Forgiveness [*kshama*] is Brahma [God], Truth, and stored abstentious merit; forgiveness is asceticism. Forgiveness is holiness. Forgiveness binds the universe together."[4] One Hindu sutra declares that when a *raja* (king) pardons a criminal, the raja assumes the criminal's karma and must expiate it.[5] This karmic rule deterred indiscriminate pardons of the wicked.

It is fair to say that pardons are not a peculiarly Western phenomenon. I imagine they have existed in every society, to varying extents. But it is also fair to say that *American* conceptions of pardons derive from the West, and from Britain in particular.

To fully understand why pardons have become politicized, we must consider what preceded the Pardon Clause, the range of alternatives available to our Constitution's framers, and why some found the clause alarming. Our modern predicament was not a bolt from the blue. Rather, it has deep roots in the past, stemming from the contested choices of our Founding Fathers.

Why the Constitution Grants a Pardon Power

Before we dive into the clause's creation, consider an antecedent question: Why a pardon power? We gain insights about the proper and improper uses of a pardon power when we consider the reasons that American governments continue to have a pardon power. To this day, every state has a clemency process, albeit one often more constrained than the federal pardon power.[6]

Mercy

In Britain, pardons were linked with mercy, for they could temper the systematic severity found in criminal laws.[7] The Crown, by dispensing mercy, came to be seen as an embodiment of forgiveness. At coronations, English monarchs bear symbols of mercy. The monarch carries a "Sword of Mercy," one with a blunt tip. Perhaps the bluntness connotes mercy, because a sword certainly does not. The monarch also carries a "Rod of Equity and Mercy," consisting of a dove atop a scepter.[8] The coronation oath of British monarchs requires them to "cause Law and Justice, in Mercy, to be Executed." Justice must be leavened with mercy. In the eighteenth century William Blackstone, an expert on the British Constitution, wrote that the monarch "has it in his power to extend mercy, wherever he thinks it is deserved."[9]

The link with mercy continued in America. General George Washington's "General Order" of September 22, 1775, declared that over a dozen mutineers were to be whipped and many others fined. But that order also granted "mercy" to three. And, according to one witness, on the day of the scheduled lashing, only one person was flogged.[10] A small dose of forgiveness presaged a heap of mercy.

Calibration

Clemency can better fit the punishment to the crime. Laws are written in general terms, often unable to draw fine distinctions among the guilty. Yet many supposed that some differences mattered in ways that a law could never quite capture. As Blackstone put it, "no man will seriously avow, that the situation and circumstances of the offender (though they alter not the essence of the crime) ought to make no distinction in the punishment."[11] Due to variations in circumstances across offenders, the same crime might call for different penalties.

Americans also saw the need for calibration. For instance, an early American court-martial convicted soldiers but also recommend mercy, citing their "Youth and Ignorance of their duty."[12] As Justice Joseph Story would later observe, no one imagined "that any system of laws can provide for every possible shade of guilt, a proportionate degree of punishment." Frequently, the proof of guilt is uncertain "not only as to the actual commission of the offence, but also, as to the aggravating or mitigating circumstances. In many cases, convictions must be founded upon presumptions and probabilities."[13] By considering shades of intent, degrees of certainty about guilt, and underlying causes, a pardoner could ensure that a punishment better fits a nuanced assessment of the entirety of the context.

Law Enforcement

It might seem paradoxical that pardons can foster compliance with the law. Pardons *undo* the punishment that the law attaches to an offense. But imagine that excessive punishment sometimes makes a criminal a more persistent offender and causes them to harden their hearts. For instance, if the legislature declares that robbery is punishable by death, then some thieves will conclude that they have nothing to lose if they also commit murder. They may have much to gain, as murder may prevent their arrest. When it came to executions, Commander in Chief Washington perhaps agreed. "I am persuaded that a frequency of Executions lessens the force of them," he said.[14] Due to this belief, he pardoned many soldiers awaiting their executions.

Alternatively, some may desist from further misdeeds if they are forgiven. If a man has made an uncharacteristic mistake and would return to being a law-abiding citizen, then pardoning him might be a superior means of inculcating a fealty to the law. Washington thought as much: the frequency of his pardons, he said, "ought to operate on the gratitude of offenders to the improvement of their morals."[15] Think of it as an eighteenth-century version of *Scared Straight,* albeit for soldiers. (*Scared Straight* was a 1978 documentary in which juvenile offenders met prisoners and were taught the harshness of prison life). A pardon of a wayward soul might set him back on the path of habitual obedience to the law.

Reconciliation

Sometimes, loathing and alienation are deep and fundamental. Rebels, insurgents, and revolutionaries—call them what you will—come to view the government and its laws as unjust or oppressive. In the past, the underlying disputes have related to taxes, political representation, slavery, and race. Whatever the precise causes, some take up arms, oppose the government's writ, and commit crimes against the state. To suppress rebellions, governments wield sticks and carrots. One stick is an armed force. The carrots are healing measures. An amnesty can be a valued means of reconciling rebels. When the government pardons insurgents, it hopes that they will lay down their arms. Alexander Hamilton observed, "in seasons of insurrection or rebellion, there are often critical moments, when a well-timed offer of pardon to the insurgents or rebels may restore the tranquility of the commonwealth."[16] Forgiveness might yield peace and reconciliation.

Attachment

Federal legislators serve their voters by helping them maneuver the immense federal bureaucracy. It is called "constituent service." The voter whose cousin gets a visa, or whose father receives a Social Security check, is more apt to vote for that politician who interceded on their behalf. It might better be called "bonding with voters." Pardons can serve a similar function. Gratitude for mercy has meant that many subjects of monarchy have felt deep allegiance to their monarchs. Perhaps some Founders thought that pardons might bind citizens to their new federal government. Citizens might be grateful for mercy to friends and family and remain firmly attached to the nascent government, rejecting calls for rebellion or the allure of foreign sovereigns.

The Missing Reasons

At America's founding, the pardon power was never justified or defended as a means for the pardoner to amass a fortune or favor allies, friends, and family. But as we shall see, pardons have been used for all these purposes, and others equally troubling. While the reasons for governments to enjoy a pardon power are lofty and worthy, any tool meant for elevated purposes can be exercised for baser ones. Nonetheless, it matters that Americans advanced certain justifications and purposes of a pardon power and omitted others. That history might mean that some pardons are problematic, perhaps unconstitutional. A president who pardons solely to secure personal benefits or raise campaign funds may be violating the implicit limits of the Pardon Clause.

British Foundations

The English Crown exercised the power of pardon as early as the sixth century. Occasionally, the Crown's exercises stoked controversies, with Parliament responding by constraining the pardon power.[17] By law, certain crimes (for example, exiling British subjects) were not pardonable, and no pardon could halt an impeachment.[18]

As discussed, pardons served many high-sounding and noble objectives, like mercy, reconciliation, attachment, and so forth. But pardons also furthered many down-to-earth, practical aims. For instance, conditional pardons helped secure soldiers, exile miscreants, and fill the Crown's coffers (since people had to pay a fee to get a pardon).[19] Pardons also helped secure Parliamentary appropriations, for Parliament was generally grateful in the wake of an amnesty.[20] The Crown also wielded pardons to bestow favors on courtiers. In exchange for their access and influence, the Crown's hangers-on charged hefty fees to would-be pardon-seekers.[21] Some things never change.[22]

While the Crown could grant pardons without Parliament's approval or assistance, it sometimes would ask Parliament to enact a law as a means of publicizing an offer. These statutes offered general pardons to all who fit within the offer's criteria. The Crown itself made general offers of pardons, either with or without statutory publication, in conjunction with coronations and at the end of rebellions and war.[23] Some of these amnesties call to mind the festive pardons that might have existed in Jewish traditions. Those seeking an individual pardon would have to prove they qualified and usually pay a fee for an individual copy. Perhaps the document might dissuade a prosecutor from bringing a prosecution. But if it did not, the pardon recipient would produce the document in court in the wake of a prosecution.[24] One advantage of statutory pardons is that individuals might plead the act of indemnity itself, without having to pay a fee for an individual pardon.[25]

In American colonies, provincial governors faced far more pardon constraints than the Crown did. In some colonies, governors proposed pardons but needed a council's advice and consent. Occasionally, an executive council wielded the pardon authority, meaning the governor had but one vote. Further, some executives could pardon only after conviction; some could reprieve (but not pardon) capital offenses, with the Crown deciding whether to pardon; and some executives could not pardon heinous offenses like treason and willful murder.[26]

State Constitutions

Blackstone maintained that pardons were incompatible with democracy.[27] Americans disagreed. New York, Delaware, Maryland, and North Carolina expressly granted their chief executives the power to pardon.[28] More commonly, as in New Hampshire, Massachusetts, New Jersey, Virginia, Vermont, and Pennsylvania, the chief executive could pardon with a council's participation.[29] In South Carolina, neither the 1776 nor the 1778 constitutions contained a pardon clause. Nonetheless, the grant of "executive authority" ceded the power to pardon.[30] One of the government's first acts was a gubernatorial pardon.[31] Georgia was the most distrustful of executive pardons, choosing to vest its governor, who was advised by an executive council, with executive powers "save *only* in the case of pardons and remission of fines, which he shall in no instance grant."[32] Instead, Georgia's chief executive could "reprieve a criminal, or suspend a fine, until the meeting of the assembly, who may determine therein as they shall judge fit."[33] By 1789, however, even Georgia had come around and granted its governor the power to pardon.[34]

The state constitutions imposed various constraints. Some barred the executive from pardoning offenses prosecuted by the state's assembly.[35] Others allowed the legislature to restrain or bar pardons.[36] In Massachusetts, New Hampshire, New Jersey, and New York, no one could be pardoned without first being convicted.[37] New

York and others forbade their executives from pardoning treason or murder; they could only reprieve such offenses, leaving pardons to the legislature.[38] Many states also excepted impeachments from the pardon power.[39]

The role of assemblies warrants further scrutiny, for some of them issued pardons and amnesties.[40] Some constitutions granted the legislature the pardon power.[41] Others left it to implication by granting the executive a power to reprieve during a recess, with an implication that the legislature would make the final decision when it reconvened.[42] Still other legislatures granted pardons with no specific or indirect constitutional authorization, as when the Massachusetts legislature passed an "Act of Indemnity" for participants in Shay's Rebellion.[43] Because the Continental Congress requested state assemblies to pardon Tories, it must have believed that they could grant clemency.[44]

Pardons allowed loyalists to switch sides without fear of legal punishment.[45] Similarly, they helped reconcile individuals seeking to secede from states.[46] They also served as a means of mitigating harsh punishments.[47] Virginia Governor Patrick Henry, for instance, pardoned individuals facing execution on the condition that they labor for the city of Richmond.[48] Finally, pardons were a means of gathering information about the enemy, as when one enemy spy received three reprieves for revealing secrets.[49]

The Continental Congress

For the states in their collective capacity, the foundational document was the Articles of Confederation. Its principal institution was the Continental Congress.[50] Don't be fooled by the name, for it resembled our Congress in name only. The Continental Congress was akin to the United Nations. While each "sovereign state" might send multiple "delegates," each state could cast but one vote in the proceedings. The Continental Congress had scant legislative powers, could not tax anyone or raise armies, and relied on states to provide money and men. It was principally an executive institution, with authority over war, foreign affairs, and the officers of the proto-national government.[51] Though it lacked an express power to forgive, the Congress pardoned offenses against the United States.[52] Concluding that others might better positioned to pardon soldiers and sailors, it delegated clemency authority to its two commanders in chief (army and navy) and other senior officers.[53]

As the earlier discussion suggested, the commander in chief of the Continental Army dispensed pardons with remarkable frequency, and his pardons served multiple purposes. Sometimes Washington sought to deter *and* grant mercy. Washington, having approved a death sentence, would sometimes allow the process to proceed even to the point that nooses were placed around necks. A last-minute pardon or reprieve would issue, with the mercy conveyed by galloping horsemen. But that pardon or reprieve might go to only nine of ten men, leaving the unlucky tenth to serve as a vivid example.[54] The point was to teach soldiers to honor the law and to have them recognize that failure to do so might result in severe consequences. Washington also pardoned in the wake of mutinies, as when he pardoned dozens of rioters, save for one lone miscreant.[55] Finally, Washington sometimes mimicked the celebratory English pardons, as when he granted a general pardon to commemorate the 1778 alliance with the French, the treaty that made France an ally against Britain.[56] Festive pardons raise fascinating questions about the scope of our Pardon Clause.

Proposing a Pardon Power

Little more than a decade after the inauguration of the Continental Congress, Americans decided that a more vigorous central government was essential. That government needed additional powers and new institutions to wield them. Many sought a separation of powers, where an energetic executive and independent judiciary would counterbalance an invigorated and more powerful legislature. To make those desires a reality, numerous state legislatures sent delegations to Philadelphia in a bid to amend the Articles of Confederation. They met in late May of 1787. Rather than merely tinkering with the Articles, the delegates quickly resolved to create a novel and grander foundation. Over the summer, marked by spirited debates and twists and turns, they offered alternative constitutional visions for the new system.

The Virginia Plan—drawn up by delegates from the Old Dominion—envisioned refashioning Congress as a legislature with great lawmaking powers. Further, the plan transferred the "executive rights" or "executive powers" of the Continental Congress to a new and independent executive, one separate from Congress.[57] Though there was no express pardon grant, because the plan envisioned transferring executive authority to the new executive, that authority would have encompassed a pardon power. In that era, the power to grant clemency was widely seen as an executive authority. Alexander Hamilton's constitutional blueprint expressly granted a pardon power to a new executive. His plan had one exception: to pardon treason would require Senate consent.[58] The New Jersey Plan—reflecting the views of smaller states—neither expressly conveyed a pardon power nor granted a generic executive power.[59]

No discussion of the pardon power ensued until the Convention took up a committee proposal in late August. Upon seeing the proposal for a pardon power vested in the president, one delegate sought to limit the power to reprieves, with pardons issuing only after the Senate's consent.[60] The president could delay, but not forgive, punishment. That proposal went nowhere. Another delegate successfully proposed that pardons be barred "in cases of impeachment," a limitation resembling the English 1700 Act of Settlement (more on that later).[61] Proposals to bar pardons before conviction or for treason lacked majority support.[62] The last idea generated some discussion, with a few delegates insisting that the president might be part of a plot to overthrow the Constitution and hence should be unable to pardon his co-conspirators.[63]

Ratifying the Pardon Clause

After finalizing the Constitution in September of 1787, the delegates sent the proposal (for that's all it was) to the Continental Congress. Congress forwarded the proposal to the states, declaring that popular conventions would decide its fate. This meant that voters in each state would choose delegates to a state convention that would determine whether the state would ratify the Constitution. If nine states ratified, it would become law, but only for those states that ratified.

While the Constitution was up for debate, intense arguments played out in pamphlets, newspapers, and convention halls. Foes of ratification—styled the Anti-Federalists because they opposed the Constitution—voiced serious objections to the presidency, insisting that the president resembled a king. There was no crown or throne, but the president would execute the law, appoint officers, make treaties, and wield a veto over proposed laws. Save for the name, where does "the president" differ from the British King, asked the Anti-Federalists.[64] They had a point.

One authority cited as evidence of that semblance was the pardon power. The complaints took on different complexions. Some said the clause gave the president "absolute power" and "unrestrained power" to pardon.[65] Others protested that the power was "too unlimited." The Pardon Clause was a howler of a mistake, it was said, for the power of clemency should be cabined by "proper restrictions," ones conspicuously absent.[66]

Luther Martin had been a delegate to the Philadelphia Convention but departed early because he opposed the Constitution. In a speech to the Maryland Legislature, Martin recounted intense apprehensions: "The power given to the president of granting reprieves and pardons, was also thought extremely dangerous." Why? The president could pardon those "guilty of treason, as well as of other offences." A president might "attempt to assume . . . powers not given by the constitution, and establish himself in regal authority." By dispensing pardons to his co-conspirators, he could "secure from punishment the creatures of his ambition, the . . . abettors of his treasonable practices."[67]

Other opponents also prophesied squalid schemes. George Mason of Virginia (who refused to sign the Constitution at Philadelphia) objected that pardons "may be sometimes exercised to screen from punishment those whom [the president] . . . instigated" and "thereby *prevent a discovery of his own guilt.*"[68] Mason had preemptive pardons in mind, ones that would preclude a trial and thus the possible airing of presidential perfidy. Another detractor feared the effect that pardons would have on rights: The president might "skreen from punishment the most treasonable attempts on the liberties of the people."[69] A North Carolinian protested that the president might lead "a combination against the rights of the people, and may reprieve or pardon [his clique]. . . . [The pardon power] may be exercised to the public good, but may also be perverted to a different [sinister] purpose."[70]

Federalists could not deny that the pardon power might be abused, for the authority had long been misused. But they made the best of it. Writing as "Marcus," James Iredell supplied soothing answers. Every "well regulated government" needed a pardon power and most thought it best placed in one person's hands. Furthermore, because presidents were unlikely to be traitors, America should not constrain the pardon power because of some "remote and improbable danger." With a touch of realism, Iredell observed that America would "have to chuse between inconveniences of some sort or other, since no institution of man can be entirely free from all." Yes, the president might use the pardon power to screen treason. But if the president needed Congress's approval before pardoning treason, as some demanded, he could not pardon America's spies and other innocents.[71]

"A Native of Virginia" made similar moves. The pardon power belonged "to the Executive branch of government; and could be placed in no other hands with propriety." Laws could not "provide for every case that may happen," meaning that some laws would be too general and lack needful exceptions. Furthermore, "So long as punishments shall continue disproportionate to crimes, the power of pardoning should some where exist."[72] In other words, if legislatures made punishments harsh, as was their wont, someone had to be able to mitigate the penalties.

Alexander Hamilton's defense is famous. "Humanity and good policy conspire to dictate," that the "benign" pardon power should be relatively unconstrained. Why? Every nation's criminal code "partakes so much of necessary severity, that without an easy access to exceptions" in the form of clemency "justice would wear a countenance too sanguinary and cruel."[73] One man could deftly dispense pardons, for he would understand "that the fate of a fellow creature depended on his *sole fiat*," a recognition that would "inspire scrupulousness and caution." At the same time, the fear "of being accused of weakness or connivance would beget equal circumspection" of a different sort.[74]

Yet not even Hamilton would deny that the Anti-Federalists had a formidable point regarding treason. Pardoning treason was fraught with troubles.

I shall not deny that there are strong reasons to be assigned for requiring [in the case of treason] the concurrence of [the Congress] or of a part of it. As treason is a crime levelled at the immediate being of the society . . . there seems a fitness in refering the expediency of an act of mercy . . . to the judgment of the Legislature. And this ought the rather to be the case, as the supposition of the connivance of the Chief Magistrate ought not be entirely excluded.[75]

This was Hamilton sheepishly admitting that the executive might try to subvert the Constitution. Recall that his Convention proposal would have denied the president an absolute power to pardon treason. Still, the grant of a pardon power to a single person had many points in its favor, certainly when compared to vesting the power in an assembly.

> It is not to be doubted that a single man of prudence and good sense, is better fitted, in delicate conjunctures, to balance the motives, which may plead for and against the remission of the punishment, than any numerous body whatever. . . . But the principal arguments for reposing the power of pardoning in . . . the Chief Magistrate is this—In seasons of insurrection or rebellion, there are often critical moments, when a well timed offer of pardon to the insurgents or rebels may restore the tranquility of the commonwealth. . . . The dilatory process of convening the Legislature . . . for the purpose of obtaining its sanction to the [pardon], would frequently be the occasion of letting slip the golden opportunity. The loss of a week, a day, an hour, may sometimes be fatal.[76]

Legislating took time, and legislatures were rarely in session. Yet, the need for a pardon might be pressing, particularly in cases of rebellion. Only the executive could act in a timely and speedy manner.

Despite the undoubted force of the Anti-Federalist arguments, only two groups proposed pardon amendments. The New York ratifying convention formally recommended that the Constitution be amended to provide that the president could pardon treason only with Congress's consent.[77] In Pennsylvania, a minority of its ratifying convention suggested that pardons would vest only after the president secured the approval of a council.[78] Congress never proposed these suggested amendments.

The defenders of the Pardon Clause won the day in the sense that every state (eventually) ratified the Constitution. Yet, because the question was whether to ratify (or not) the entire Constitution, we can never quite know whether the Anti-Federalists had the better argument. Recall that several Federalists conceded points here, whereas on other matters relating to the Constitution, they often conceded nothing. Had states voted clause by clause, some of them might have spurned the Pardon Clause. For all we know, state conventions might have ratified the Constitution *despite* the clause's broad grant of clemency authority.

Both the opponents and the defenders of the Pardon Clause were prescient. They foresaw many vexing issues arising from granting an almost limitless pardon power, and over our nation's rich history, we have seen these prophecies bear fruit.

CHAPTER 2

Parsing the Pardon Power

D URING THE CIVIL WAR, Abraham Lincoln sometimes issued epigrammatic pardons, writings lacking the formalities typically found in grants of clemency. On the reverse of a letter requesting the release of a Confederate soldier, Lincoln scribbled "Let it be done."[1] That did the trick. On another request, this time for a member of the Rebel Maryland Artillery, the president was more verbose: "Let this man take the oath of [loyalty] and be discharged" from confinement.[2] Lincoln knew how to get to the point, as his Gettysburg Address well proved. The significance to the pardon recipient was enormous, even as the scribbling was short.

Like some of Lincoln's pardons, the Pardon Clause is deceptively short. Found at the end of Section 2 of Article II of the Constitution, the clause declares that "*he shall have Power to grant Reprieves and Pardons for Offences against the United States, except in Cases of Impeachment.*"[3] This clause covers a vast ground and invests the president with immense exemptive and immunizing authority. The president can undo any penalty attached to an offense and thus can forgive many (though not all) violations of federal law.

To see why the pardon pen has become such a potent instrument of politics, we must first grasp some basics—the exceptions and limits of the pardon power, but especially its astonishing breadth. This chapter does that by considering the clause's twenty words. Sometimes, the difficulties and complexities of interpretation are inversely related to the number of words. The shorter the clause, the more we must interpret, decode, and infer. Of course, we are not the first to mull over these charged words, for

16

we follow in the footsteps of many courts and presidents who have done the same.

Reprieves

Let's start with reprieves. Reprieves are a narrow form of clemency. As the Supreme Court put it, a *reprieve* is a "delay [of] a judicial sentence when the president shall think the merits of the case, or some cause connected with the offender, may require [the deferral]."[4] Sometimes, the temporary delay occurs before the sentence begins. The president might reprieve a death sentence, thereby barring an execution for the time being. At other times, the delay occurs during a prison sentence, as when a jailer temporarily releases a reprieved prisoner. When the reprieve ends, the prisoner must return to jail. Of course, a follow-on pardon makes reconfinement unnecessary.

The Supreme Court has cited two situations where reprieves might be appropriate: pregnancy and the onset of insanity.[5] The court supposed that it would be improper to punish under these circumstances.[6] Other reasons for issuing a reprieve might include reviewing new evidence of innocence, awaiting the results of an appeal, or suspending punishment while the president considers a pardon. Whenever a delay would be useful, reprieves are fitting.

Pardons

Whereas reprieves are relatively uncomplicated, pardons are multifaceted. A single word can signal so much. The Supreme Court once declared that a "pardon is an act of grace, proceeding from the power entrusted with the execution of the laws, which exempts the individual on whom it is bestowed from the punishment the law inflicts for a crime he has committed."[7] In modern English, the president, who has constitutional power to execute the laws, may exempt an offender from the law's sanctions.

Within "pardons" are a host of auxiliary powers and permutations. Below are some concepts that have long been understood to be integral to the pardon power. The vast array of choices generates the complexity and breadth.

A *full pardon* declares that any punishment must cease. This far-reaching immunity is often what comes to mind when one discusses a "pardon." The Supreme Court once said that a full pardon "blots out of existence the guilt" and makes the recipient a "new man."[8] But the court has retreated from these stances. The modern approach treats a pardon as eliminating punishment, but not necessarily *forgetting the underlying acts.* In other words, the pardon forgives, and eliminates, any sanction. But forgiveness is not a promise of forgetting.[9]

A *commutation* does not wipe away the entire sanction. Rather, it commutes—reduces—a punishment. Perhaps the commutation reduces a life sentence to ten years. Or it might moderate a fine from $20,000 to $2,000. Usually (though not always) the recipient welcomes the commutation, but for all legal purposes that person remains an offender.

A *remission* is a declaration that a person may dodge monetary and property penalties attached to their violation of the law.[10] A remission may exempt someone from having to pay a fine owed to the government. Alternatively, a remission may nullify (undo) a previous forfeiture, meaning that the government returns funds or property to the pardoned individual. Either a full pardon or a commutation may work as a remission. A full pardon restores innocence and bars the collection of fines and forfeitures and potentially remits any previously paid penalties. In contrast, a commutation leaves the guilt intact but might eliminate any unpaid penalties.

An *amnesty* (sometimes called a general pardon) is a pardon of a group. The president may issue a proclamation that, by its terms, pardons a multitude. An amnesty often helps pacify a rebellion, as in "I hereby grant to all persons who have . . . participated in the existing rebellion . . . amnesty and pardon."[11] But an amnesty need not be related to rebellions or insurrections—think President Jimmy

Carter's amnesty for Vietnam draft dodgers. An amnesty is by its nature indiscriminate, because the president pays no attention to an offender's personal situation—guilt, innocence, service to the nation, extenuating circumstances, or anything else. Everyone in the group, however broadly defined, is pardoned for some offense even if they are otherwise reprobates.

A *preemptive pardon* is a pardon before conviction. A full pardon for murder before trial bars a murder trial of the alleged killer. This pardon precludes any prosecution or trial, possibly preventing the discovery of additional wrongdoing by the recipient and offenses by others. For an accused, a preemptive pardon is best. For the rest of society, perhaps not so much.

A *blanket pardon* forgives all offenses, covering all felonies and misdemeanors. Most pardons grant clemency for specified offenses allegedly committed by the offender, such as robbery, drug dealing, or tax evasion. In other words, most pardons list, at most, a handful of offenses. But blanket pardons are truly sweeping, forgiving all (or almost all) offenses previously committed. Specific offenses are not listed, precisely because the pardon is intended to be more comprehensive.

A *conditional pardon* is a contract, because it requires the satisfaction of conditions or stipulations. The president might promise that a pardon vests once the recipient first testifies against accomplices. Or the president might stipulate that a pardon will take effect once the individual admits guilt. These are conditions that must be satisfied before the pardon takes effect. Alternatively, the president might issue a pardon and declare that it will remain valid only so long as the recipient desists from, say, taking up arms against the government. This is a condition attached to the pardon's continuing validity. If the pardon recipient ever violates the stipulation, the original punishment springs back into existence. Because conditions can be attached to commutations, amnesties, reprieves, and remissions, each of these forms of mercy may be conditional as well. There can be conditional commutations, conditional amnesties, conditional reprieves, and so on.

Conditions have a profound impact on pardon recipients. One conditional pardon may induce a person to take an action (for example, admit guilt) to secure the benefits. Another conditional pardon may persuade its recipient to refrain from acts that would void the pardon.

We could draw more distinctions, but these suffice for now.

Offenses

The conventional view is that the word *offenses* limits the pardon power to *crimes*.[12] The president can pardon or commute criminal punishments and remit criminal fines, penalties, and forfeitures. Crimes are legal transgressions that carry significant moral condemnation. Murder, rape, theft—these are the violations that come to mind. The Constitution has special rules for the trial of *criminal* offenses, ones related to juries, evidence, prosecutions, and punishments.[13] Indeed, one reason for reading offenses as nothing but crimes is that the Fifth Amendment's Double Jeopardy Clause uses "offense" to cover *criminal* offenses. That clause declares, "nor shall any person be subject for the same offence to be twice put in jeopardy of life or limb."[14] In other words, the government cannot try you twice for the same offense. If "offense" in the Fifth Amendment refers to crimes, "offenses" must bear the same meaning in the Pardon Clause, or so the theory goes.

I think the conventional view—supposing that the pardon power excludes civil sanctions owed to the government—is mistaken. To begin with, the Fifth Amendment does not say that "offenses" refers only to crimes. It merely declares that certain offenses are subject to the double jeopardy bar—those involving life and limb. Something can be an "offense" even if it does not jeopardize life or limb.

Furthermore, the distinction between civil and criminal offenses is a modern construct. In the eighteenth century, *all* fines, penalties, and forfeitures payable to the government were offenses against the United States and, therefore, pardonable by the president.[15] At some point in the nineteenth century, the idea of "civil" fines and penalties arose.[16] I suspect it was from this innovation in categorization, and trial procedure, that the modern view arose that the pardon extends to criminal offenses and excludes civil wrongs.

You might be wondering: What *is* a civil fine or civil penalty? One thing that makes a fine or penalty "civil" as opposed to "criminal" is the *judicial process used to impose it.* Criminal trials require proof beyond a reasonable doubt. That is a very high standard of proof, one appropriate for the greater moral condemnation that attaches to a *criminal* conviction. Furthermore, the sanctions attached to criminal violations can include jail time, even execution. In contrast, civil trials (usually) cannot impose imprisonment. Additionally, civil trials require merely a preponderance of evidence of wrongdoing, a sense that it is more likely than not that a person has violated the law. Accordingly, it is easier for the government to secure victory as a plaintiff in a civil lawsuit than it would be as a prosecutor in a criminal case.

In my view, the pardon power attaches regardless of the type of trial, the amount of moral censure that attaches, or the label attached to the transgression. Obviously, when the government can imprison a person, the underlying transgression is pardonable. But any fine, penalty, or forfeiture payable to the federal government signals that a person has transgressed the law and offended the United States. Per this argument, the term *offenses* means *legal transgressions,* and "against the United States" means that the offenses breach obligations to the federal government. Put another way, the phrase "offenses against the United States" encompasses *any* violation of federal law where public interests predominate—that is, where Congress has authorized governmental action against the offender, including lawsuits to collect fines and penalties payable to the federal government. It could be a tax fine (for the late filing of a return), a labor penalty (for an employer violating federal labor rules), or a property forfeiture (for using a car for illicit purposes). Without regard to whether the fine, penalty, or forfeiture is grounded in a criminal conviction, the payment to the United States signals that the United States is aggrieved and *offended* by the conduct.

Supreme Court decisions and early practices endorse a broad reading of "offenses." In an 1885 case, *The Laura,* the court declared that the president "may remit [forgive] fines, penalties, and forfeitures of *every description* arising under the laws of Congress."[17] The Supreme Court seems to have said that the president may pardon all sanctions payable to the government, whether collected via a criminal prosecution or a civil lawsuit. This reading reflects commonsense, for as Justice Neil Gorsuch has observed in another context, civil penalties are "sometimes more severely punitive than the parallel criminal sanctions *for the same conduct.*"[18] A civil fine of $10 million is far more punitive than a criminal penalty of $100. It would be anomalous to suppose that while the president may pardon a criminal penalty, he cannot pardon a civil fine.

Noah Messing has conducted the most extensive and sophisticated study of civil fines, penalties, and forfeitures paid (or payable) to the government.[19] He demonstrates that in England and her American colonies, the pardon power covered all sanctions owed to the government, sanctions that included what we call civil fines, penalties, and forfeitures.[20] Messing also points out that Presidents Washington, Adams, and Jefferson—our first presidents—pardoned offenses that might today be deemed civil. They forgave breaches of revenue laws, illegal importations of goods, and failure to secure proper licenses.[21]

In short, whether Congress labels an offense civil or criminal does not matter, for the president can remit any fine, penalty, or forfeiture owed to the United States, regardless of the process used to collect it or the burden of proof at trial.

Unpardonable Wrongs

Not every violation of federal law constitutes an "offense against the United States" that the president may forgive. Some federal laws recognize offenses against private parties. If Sally hits Wanda, the president cannot pardon Sally's wrong to Wanda. Wanda has an action for "battery" against Sally that the president cannot disturb. If Subbulaxmi trespasses on Frank's land to pick some flowers, the president cannot forgive that trespass, meaning that Frank may sue Subbulaxmi for damages. The United States might have created (or recognized) these offenses against private parties, but they are not offenses against the United States.

A broader category is at work here. As William Blackstone noted, where concerns for private justice predominate, the pardon power has no application.[22] While there is an element of public interest in every wrong (else why empower the courts to hear cases seeking redress for such wrongs), *private interests predominate in private wrongs.* For good reason, the president cannot pardon a private trespass or private breach of contract because in these situations, the private injury predominates. Again, if Sally has wronged Wanda, the United States is in no position to forgive. Wanda might forgive, after a payment or an apology, but the president cannot absolve.

There is an analogous pardon exception, one where a *private party acquires an interest from the government.* This gets complicated and interesting. Sometimes, when Congress creates an offense with a fine, penalty, or forfeiture payable to the government, it authorizes private persons to bring a lawsuit to collect. For instance, Congress penalizes government contractors who submit false expense claims and permits private parties to bring lawsuits on behalf of the federal government. If the party proves that the contractor defrauded the government, it has a right to keep at least 15 percent of any amounts collected.[23] The federal government is essentially offering a bounty for prevailing in a lawsuit against those who offended the government. Lawyers refer to these sorts of legal actions *as informer or qui tam suits.* In essence, people may sue on behalf of the government, *and themselves,* and keep a portion of any monies and property collected.

Based on longstanding principles, the president cannot pardon fines due to someone who has sued on behalf of the government. Although prior to the commencement of a lawsuit, the president could have pardoned the entire fine or forfeiture due to the federal government, once a private party brings a suit on behalf of the government, she acquires a private interest in the suit that the president cannot pardon.[24] This was an enduring British rule that preserved the incentives of persons to bring and successfully prosecute lawsuits on behalf of the government. Private parties would be far less inclined to investigate and file suits if they knew that their financial interests in government fines could be compromised by pardons. Hence, to encourage their efforts, while still permitting pardons, courts concluded that the executive could not extinguish a private person's interest in a fine owed to the government after the person had sued on behalf of the government. The Crown could pardon the government's interest, but not the private interest. This traditional limitation on the pardon power likewise applies in America, for there is no reason to suppose that the Constitution (or its founders) meant to depart from this sensible constraint on the pardon prerogative.[25]

Another category of offenses that the president cannot pardon is a *continuing* offense. Although the executive may pardon fines associated with a public nuisance, say a polluting factory, the executive cannot sanction the continuous pollution.[26] In other words, the president cannot grant someone a license to pollute because she cannot use the pardon power to authorize ongoing violations of federal law.

Finally, the category of private wrongs has a broader scope than some might imagine, as it prevents the president from releasing certain individuals from jail. For instance, the president cannot pardon civil contempt of court. Contempt of court is a sanction against insolent or disobedient parties before the court. Civil contempt arises when a party in a civil dispute refuses to obey a court decree. For instance, a party might refuse to pay court-ordered alimony. In this case, the court may order a fine or imprisonment. The person in jail for civil contempt can secure release as soon as she complies with the court order. Because the *civil contempt* sanction is for the benefit of a private party, the president cannot pardon it. This is a longstanding limitation from Britain that the Supreme Court has upheld. Yet when the contempt is to vindicate the interest of the United States—so-called criminal contempt—the president can pardon the jail time or fine.[27]

A pattern emerges. When the interests being vindicated are primarily private interests, the president cannot reprieve, commute, or pardon. However, when the wrong is committed against the United States, and thus there is a wrong that the nation may forgive, the president can choose to absolve and relieve someone of imprisonment, fines, penalties, and forfeitures.

Offenses, Offenders, and the Innocent

To say that the president can forgive *offenses,* as the Constitution does, is to declare that the president can pardon *offenders*—people who have transgressed the laws. That is perhaps why some have suggested that accepting a pardon or commutation is an implicit admission of guilt. For some, the acceptance of a pardon or a commutation, to stave off trial or to seek release from jail, signals that the recipient is *guilty of the offense.* In fact, the Supreme Court has said that the issuance of a pardon "carries an imputation of guilt."[28] The president must believe the recipient is guilty. Further, "acceptance [of the pardon by a person is] a confession of it."[29] Anyone who pleads a pardon or welcomes it has implicitly admitted their guilt.

The court overclaimed. The president can grant clemency to the innocent, a power grounded in common sense and history. The power to pardon must encompass the innocent, as a moment's reflection will show. Imagine two men on death row. One is guilty by admission. The other maintains his spotless innocence, and the president fully believes him so. How can it be that the president can pardon the guilty man but not the innocent? In comparison to the guilty individual, the innocent victim is far more deserving. Consistent with commonsense, pardons have long benefited those who insist upon their innocence and whom the pardoner—king, queen, general, governor—believes is blameless.

What does this mean for how we view pardon recipients? As a matter of logic, the issuance of a pardon does not imply that the president regards the person as guilty. Likewise, someone who utilizes the pardon to leave jail or avoid a penalty has not thereby conceded their culpability. Nonetheless, because most pardon recipients are guilty, people will continue to suppose that a pardon recipient is blameworthy and implicitly admitting as much. So, while pardons do not logically imply guilt, many people will nonetheless draw that inference.

Against the United States

The president can forgive transgressions *against the entire nation.* No one doubts that this phrase excludes state offences, for when the Constitution uses the phrase "United States" it means to cover the federal government created by the Constitution and not the individual states that compose the union. Hence the president cannot forgive violations of Maine or Montana law.

The pardon power extends to offenses against the United States, wherever they may occur, including the high seas and overseas. If anyone, whether a citizen or not, commits an act of piracy on the ocean, the president can forgive the offense (the United States claims jurisdiction over any pirate). If an American citizen commits a federal drug crime in Thailand, the president can forgive it. Finally, the pardon power extends to the territories and the District of Columbia, as offenses in those areas are also considered against the United States.

Except in Cases of Impeachment

While the British Crown could pardon, some acts of clemency stirred great controversies. Over time, Parliament constrained the power by statute. By the eighteenth century, Parliament had barred the Crown from pardoning those officials who exiled subjects overseas[30] *and* had provided that "no Pardon . . . shall be pleadable to an Impeachment by the Commons in Parliament."[31]

The impeachment exception to the Crown's pardon power is of interest because it casts light on the Pardon Clause's impeachment exception. Impeachment is an exceedingly fascinating constitutional mechanism. Under the US Constitution, impeachment is a means of policing who may continue to serve as an officer of the United States. Officers may be removed and barred from future service if they have committed "treason, bribery, or other high crimes and misdemeanors."[32] Our impeachment process never imposes imprisonment, much less corporal or capital punishment. By contrast, in England (and then Britain), impeachment was a means of punishing *anyone, with jail time, even death.* Ordinary subjects, officers, and legislators were punished via an impeachment in the House of Commons and a trial in the House of Lords.[33] Hence in England impeachment was a far more significant legislative tool.

The British impeachment constraint—"no pardon shall be pleadable to an impeachment"—arose after a bruising impeachment storm. During the reign of Charles II, a damaging letter from the Earl of Danby to the French monarch surfaced in Parliament amidst fears of a supposed Catholic conspiracy.[34] Enraged by the Earl's attempt to broker a peace with Catholic France, the Commons impeached him.[35] Charles II played hardball, dissolving the Parliament.[36] Charles thought the dissolution of Parliament had also dissolved the impeachment. The Commons would have to begin from square one, with the possibility of a new dissolution always looming.

After the election of the new Parliament, the impeachment proceedings continued. Seeing this, Charles pardoned Danby, hoping to terminate the proceedings once and for all. In response, the House of Commons stoutly denied that a pardon could halt an impeachment.[37] But a trial in the House of Lords never took place, and the Earl's standing eventually recovered.[38] Nonetheless, the Commons prevailed on the principle. In the Act of Settlement, passed years later, Parliament declared that "no Pardon . . . [shall] be pleadable to an Impeachment by the Commons in Parliament."[39] This meant that someone could not use a pardon to terminate impeachment proceedings. This was a momentous change, for no King or Queen could halt an impeachment and prevent the discovery of wrongdoing by the Crown or its ministers.

The Constitution's impeachment exception is more sweeping, for unlike the English rule, the Constitution's exception bars pardons even in the wake of a *Senate conviction.* The Act of Settlement's peculiar language did not bar pardons *after* an impeachment conviction in the House of Lords. It merely barred pardons that sought to terminate impeachment proceedings. Indeed, in 1715, King George pardoned three Scottish Lords whom the House of Lords had previously sentenced to death.[40] Under the Constitution, however, the president cannot pardon the effects of a Senate conviction. The broader exception—"in cases of impeachment" rather than "pleadable to an impeachment by the [House of] Commons"—signals that the president can do nothing to halt the impeachment process. He cannot terminate a House impeachment proceeding or a Senate trial. Nor can the president shield officers from the effects of a Senate impeachment conviction. If the Senate ousts someone from office, the president has no means of shielding that officer from the ignominy of the conviction or its consequences.[41]

Our Constitution's broader constraint on pardons makes eminent sense. Given the narrow sanctions that the Senate may impose (removal from office and a bar on future officeholding), clemency seems unnecessary in the wake of a Senate conviction.[42] Compared to impeachment in Britain, where lives were in the balance (impeachment and conviction could lead to execution), much less is at issue in an impeachment under the Constitution. Given the far lower stakes, it makes less sense to permit presidential pardons after a Senate conviction. Furthermore, because the House prosecutes the impeachment before the Senate, it wields the executive power of prosecution over high crimes and misdemeanors.[43] In Senate trials, the House (rather than the president) acts to vindicate the *nation's* interest. All in all, the Founders thought that the president should be unable to use pardons to shield officers from impeachment and removal.

He Shall Have Power to Grant

The Constitution grants all this power (and more!) to the president. As noted earlier, some people at the Founding believed it was suitable to have one person be the dispenser of mercy. Without the nod of anyone else, the president may decide whom to reprieve, pardon, and commute. And the president may determine the conditions, if any, to attach to these forms of clemency—for example, paying fines, admitting guilt, laying down arms, and so on. Some guilty people will never be punished and may even avoid prosecution. Others may be punished far less severely than federal law demands, for a ten-year term might be commuted to time served, with the miscreant released from jail immediately.

Can anyone else, besides the president, grant pardons and reprieves? The Pardon Clause never implies that anyone else may do so; it is focused on the president. But by the same token, the Constitution never quite declares that no one else may dispense clemency. We will return to this point later, for it has profound implications for pardon reform.

An Early Pardon

Going through the clause to introduce the fundamentals is valuable. But it would be especially illuminating to *see* a pardon. I have selected one from George Washington. With some exceptions, this one is rather akin to thousands that followed.

To all persons to whom these presents shall come
—Greeting.

whereas, Joseph Hood late of the Massachusetts district mariner, at a Circuit Court of the United States, lately holden in and for the said Massachusetts district was lately convicted of the crime of Manslaughter committed on the high seas and within the jurisdiction of the same Court and by the Judgment the said Joseph Hood was sentenced and adjudged to suffer eighteen months imprisonment, to pay to the use of the United States the sum of five hundred dollars and to stand committed until the said Judgement of the Court was complied with, and whereas the said Joseph Hood hath by his petition to me set forth that he has already sustained an imprisonment of many months before his trial and hath an aged mother to maintain, and the character and conduct of the said Joseph Hood is certified to be otherwise fair and honest, and the said Joseph Hood by his said petition hath besought a remission of so much of the said Judgment of the Court as subjects him to further imprisonment. Therefore I George Washington President of the United States, in consideration of the premises herein before set forth have thought proper and by these presents do grant unto the said Joseph Hood a full, free and entire pardon of the said offence whereof he so stands convicted so far as the same relates to the further term of imprisonment part of the Judgment of the said Court and not otherwise hereby willing and requiring that when and as soon as the said Joseph Hood shall have satisfied the Judgment of the said Court as far as the same relates to the fine and costs of prosecution on him imposed to be forthwith discharged from Custody.

In Testimony whereof, I have caused the Seall of the United States of America to be affixed to these presents, and signed the same with my hand. Done at the City of Philadelphia the second day of January, 1796 and of the Independence of the United States of America the twentieth.

G[eorge]Washington,
By the President,
Timothy Pickering
Secretary of State[44]

There is a great deal going on here. To begin with, the pardon *was not addressed to the pardoned.* It was addressed to the world: Whoever reads this—greeting! This made sense because the most important readers would include judges, prosecutors, and jailers. The pardon then described the person, trial, offense, and punishment, the better to ensure that only the *proper* Joseph Hood received its benefits. Though it promised a "full, free, and entire pardon," there were strings attached. Hood would be discharged from prison only after he paid the imposed fine and the costs of the prosecution. This was really a partial commutation. This is often a problem with pardons. They use certain words or phrases—such as "full pardon"—that might imply one thing but mean something else when one reads the entire document. Furthermore, the pardon turned on certain "premises . . . set forth" about the situation. The pardon was issued in light of the crime, that Hood had been in prison for a while, Hood's general character, and his mother's need of assistance. Under English law, if the Crown had been deceived, the pardon was rendered invalid.[45] Perhaps the same rule applied to presidential pardons—in which case, declaring the reasons might be especially useful. Finally, the pardon ends with signatures and a seal. These signs of authentication proved to the world that George Washington had pardoned Joseph Hood.

* * *

Understanding some fundamentals makes it easier to grasp how presidents might abuse the pardon pen. Hopefully, one can better see how presidents might misuse their pardon power by showering mercy on zealous allies, attaching troubling conditions on an amnesty, or granting clemency to secure the votes of grateful recipients and their friends and families.

We turn to history under the Pardon Clause. We first take up an exemplar, George Washington. We then slide into a long history of questionable, even wrongful grants of clemency.

Sometimes, the impact of a constitutional provision grows over time, meaning its weight and implications are initially overlooked by many. Such provisions may have seemed inconsequential, for the Founders could not have foreseen how vital they might become in the future. As Chapter 1 made clear, however, that cannot be said of the pardon power, for it never seemed minor or innocuous. To borrow from Justice Antonin Scalia, this "wolf c[ame] as a wolf," leading many to dread the power the Constitution vested in one man.[46] Indeed, the Pardon Clause had legions of early detractors. The course of American history suggests that the critics had a point, for there have been abuses of the awesome power to forgive offenses against the United States.

CHAPTER 3

Washingtonian Mercy

FIRST IMPRESSIONS MATTER. First *constitutional* impressions matter, too. George Washington was keenly aware that early practices mattered, for posterity would look to the past to make sense of the Constitution. Even the most minor issue might become momentous, he told John Adams. "Many things which appear of little importance in themselves and at the beginning, may have great and durable consequences from their having been established at the commencement of a new general government."[1] Washington sought the Constitution's true meaning and to implement that meaning. "As the first of every thing, in our situation will serve to establish a Precedent," he advised James Madison, "it is devoutly wished on my part, that these precedents may be fixed on true principles."[2] He knew that his actions would serve as precedents for decades, perhaps centuries, and that his influence would be greatest on the presidency: "I walk on untrodden ground. There is scarcely an action, the motive of which may not be subject to a double interpretation. There is scarcely any part of my conduct, which may not hereafter be drawn into precedent."[3]

When it came to pardons, Washington was hardly a greenhorn. Recall that he had energetically wielded the pardon pen as commander in chief of the Continental Army. He had often leavened severe punishment with conspicuous grants of mercy. As president, Washington knew that not everyone warranted clemency. But some received it, and we can learn much from Washington's motives, justifications, and practices as they help illuminate the Pardon Clause.

The Process

Washington prized method and deliberation. He sought the advice of others about the best interpretation of a treaty, whether to sign a bill, and whom to appoint.[4] That careful, methodical, and wise approach extended to pardons. As remains true today, individuals wrote to the president seeking a pardon. Faced with a request, Washington often sought (or received) advice from the US attorney who had prosecuted the case and the presiding judge.[5] They would be most familiar with the petitioner and the circumstances of the crime and trial. They could best address contrition, intent, mistake, extenuating circumstances, and so on. The president often sought the advice of his cabinet members, too, including the attorney general.[6] On one occasion, he sought and received the counsel of Chief Justice John Jay.[7]

This consultative process took time. Applications came by mail. The president would then write letters to others and seek their advice. After receiving advice, often delivered again via the mail, he would deliberate. Sometimes, there was a sense of urgency, as when a prisoner was to be executed soon. Even here, the president might grant a reprieve to give himself more time.[8] But occasionally, the trial court would delay issuing a judgment precisely to provide the defendant with time to apply for a pardon. Far more than many might imagine, the executive power of pardoning was exercised with the assistance of federal judges, who supplied time, information, and opinions. It was not quite collaborative, for the president held the power and exercised it as he saw fit. But he was keenly interested in what others with greater information thought about the applicant, a practice and depth of consideration that made eminent sense.

The First Denial

The new government, established under the Constitution, was up and running in 1789. Congress passed criminal laws, including laws regulating crime on American ships. In 1790, the federal government charged Thomas Bird with murder. Bird, an Englishman, had been a crew member of the sloop *Mary,* which left England in 1787 with seven on board, including Captain John Connor. The vessel sailed first to the Guinean Coast to purchase slaves. According to Bird, Captain Connor had brutalized crew members, one of whom died. Bird also claimed that Connor had beaten him with a water pump handle and ropes. Fearing further brutality, Bird and others shot and killed Captain Conner off the coast of Africa. The *Mary* unhurriedly made its way to Boston, arriving in the summer of 1789. Upon discovering the ship, officials learned of the murder. After a year in confinement, Bird and one other sailor were indicted by a grand jury. A jury found Bird guilty and sentenced him to death, with the execution set for June 25, 1790.[9]

On June 5, Bird sent a dictated letter to the president saying that "the fatal sentence . . . rings in my Ears & harrows up my soul. . . . The time is short Great Washington, too short, for a wretch harden'd in Crimes to prepare for that Country, from whose bourn no Traveller e'ver return'd." Please grant "a Pardon or Commute the punishment to something, to any thing, short of Death," wrote Bird. Evidently, someone knew quite a bit about the pardon power, as the petition proves: "It is usual for Kings and Emperors, at the Commencement of their Reign to grant such indulgences, Permit me then to beg that the Commencement of your administration may be marked, by Extending mercy to the first Condemned [to death] under it." Bird added, "my Case demands [your] immediate attention." Listen, he pleaded, "to the cries, of a wretch, who unless your Excellency interpose will . . . [soon] be beyond the reach of your Excellency's goodness."[10] It is hard not to be moved.

The presiding judge, who thought Bird's case was the nation's first capital trial, sent Washington the underlying details, including his sense "that the Charge appeared fully proved."[11] The president sought the opinion of Supreme Court Chief Justice John Jay, wondering, "would there be prudence, justice or policy in extending mercy"?[12]

Jay replied: "There does not appear to be a single Circumstance in the case of the murderer in question, to recommend a Pardon—His own Petition contains no averment of Innocence, no Palliative for Guilt, no complaint of Court[,] Jury or witnesses."[13]

Washington declined Bird's petition.[14] Before a crowd of over three thousand, Bird's was the first execution under the Constitution. Afterward, Washington wrote the district judge: "No palliating circumstance appeared in the case of this unhappy man to recommend him to mercy. . . . I could not therefore have justified it to the laws of my Country, had I, in this instance, exercised that pardoning power [vested in me]."[15] Washington stayed his pardon pen because he saw no extenuating circumstances.

The First Pardon

Samuel Dodge, an army veteran, was a federal customs inspector in late 1790.[16] Dodge had entered a cargo vessel that was unloading. Federal law barred unloading goods after 7 PM; the penalty for permitting such an activity consisted of a fine of $400 and ineligibility for federal office. Nonetheless, the crew unloaded molasses barrels after 7 PM. A grand jury indicted Dodge in 1791, based on facts supplied by an "informer."[17] Under federal law, informers could receive a share of any fine collected by the government. Hence, informers had a keen interest in the case. Dodge said he was "induced to plead guilty . . . trusting that the purity of his intentions" would move the president to "remit all the penalties."[18] Dodge now sought clemency from the president, raising several points: that he was ignorant of the recently enacted law, that the grand jury certified that he had not sought to defraud the government, that the public had suffered no harm, and that the judges had stayed the judgment to give the president ample time to act on his petition. Further, the federal customs collector for New York vouched for Dodge's character, and the ship's owners observed there had been light enough that night to see the offloaded cargo.[19]

Though Washington sought the advice of Attorney General Edmund Randolph, we lack the latter's opinion.[20] The president likely reached out to Alexander Hamilton, as well, for the latter requested the views of the district attorney, Richard Harrison.[21] Hamilton asked Harrison's opinion on how the pardon power interacted with the informer's right to a portion of the fine. Harrison opined that the president could "not affect the rights of individuals" and hence could not forgive the portion of any fine payable to informers.[22] The pardon could make this clear by expressly excluding the informer's portion. Or the court, in implementing the pardon, could protect the informer's portion of the fine, leaving it untouched.[23]

The president pardoned Dodge.[24] Washington also instructed the attorney general to retain the records of the court proceedings to "shew the ground upon which the said pardon was granted."[25] Several months earlier, Washington was unable to justify to "the laws of [his] country" a pardon for Thomas Bird.[26] Now, he would make sure to preserve the evidence that undergirded Dodge's pardon. Though we lack a copy of the pardon, Washington explained to Randolph that the custom inspector's "errors were unintentional."[27]

The First Amnesty

The Constitution does not explicitly mention amnesties. Nonetheless, the Pardon Clause cedes that power as part of the authority to grant pardons. An amnesty is just a mass pardon, issued to many at once.

The first amnesty occurred after the first revolt.[28] This was fitting, for when rebellions flare, pardons often are used to reconcile the insurgents. The federal government had levied a tax on distilled spirits, including whiskey. This "whiskey tax" was supposed to generate revenue to redeem federal debts. Americans, farmers especially, did not care for the tax (some things never change). These farmers had long distilled their surplus grain to make whiskey. Whiskey was easy to transport and even easier to sell. Now, the federal government was taxing that source of income.

In western Pennsylvania, opponents resorted to violence and intimidation to prevent collection. In August 1792, John Neville, the federal inspector, rented a room in Pittsburgh. After receiving threats from tax opponents, the landlord ousted Neville. Soon, anyone cooperating with tax officials faced intimidation. Collaborators might find their stills demolished or their barns ablaze.

Resistance to the tax continued through 1793. In June, Neville was burned in effigy by a mob. In November, men stormed the home of revenue collector Benjamin Wells. At gunpoint, the invaders forced him to surrender his commission. This was humiliating. A commission is addressed to the world and specifies an officer's status, title, and authority. In a manner of speaking, the rebels had sacked Wells and insulted the federal government.

Seeking to restore order, the district attorney secured subpoenas, summoning all the tax dodgers to a Philadelphia court. Initially, a US marshal was able to serve most of the subpoenas. But shots were fired at Neville and the marshal. That was the breaking point. Soon, hundreds of armed men surrounded and attacked Inspector Neville's home. During a ceasefire, a rebel was killed, leading a throng to set the house on fire and capture the marshal and the inspector.

In August, thousands gathered at Braddock's Field near Pittsburgh. There was talk of independence or uniting with Spain or Britain. Attendees lionized the ongoing French Revolution and its novel instrument of terror, the guillotine.

Washington sent commissioners to parley with the rebels. He eventually concluded that force was necessary. Washington rode at the head of a multitude, with thirteen thousand militiamen provided by the governors of Virginia, Maryland, New Jersey, and Pennsylvania. This was one of two times that a sitting president served as a field commander.[29] At some point, he left the force under the care of Virginia Governor Henry Lee.

Rebel leaders fled before the force arrived, and no confrontation ensued. More than a hundred were arrested. After asserting control over the area, Lee issued the first amnesty:

> By virtue of the powers and authority in me vested by the President of the United States, and in obedience to his benign intentions . . . I do, by this my proclamation, declare and make known to all concerned that a full, free, and entire pardon, (excepting and providing as hereafter mentioned) is hereby granted to all persons residing within the [several western counties] in the state of Pennsylvania, and in the county of Ohio, in the state of Virginia, guilty of treason, or misprision of treason against the United States, or otherwise directly or indirectly engaged in the wicked and unhappy tumults and disturbances lately existing in those counties.[30]

Lee's amnesty applied to those guilty of treason, those who failed to report treason, and those who engaged in the "wicked and unhappy tumults"—meaning it covered thousands. But the generous clemency had its limits. The proclamation expressly excluded absconders, certain named individuals, and those already facing some criminal process (such as those confronting charges or out on bail). Further, there were two other important constraints: first, any penalty for failing to pay the excise tax was not forgiven; and second, anyone who later obstructed the laws of the United States would lose the pardon's benefit. This was not quite a full, free, and *entire* pardon. This was a conditional amnesty, with a restriction tied to future behavior.

In 1795, Washington granted a broader amnesty.[31] And on his last day in office, March 3, 1797, he pardoned more of the rebels, many of whom had absconded.[32] This was the first presidential pardon on the president's last day in office.

So, the first rebellion saw not one but two amnesties. That was not uncommon, because sometimes the first offer excluded the worst rebels. And even if the promised amnesty is broad and unconditional, not all rebels will accept that first offer. In the case of the Whiskey Rebellion, the first amnesty was conditional, turning upon the future behavior of recipients. Relatedly, the first federal amnesty was issued by Governor Lee under a *delegation* from the president. The second amnesty had broader scope, but it, too, did not grant clemency to all the rebels.

The First Reprieves

In 1795, two Whiskey rebels were sentenced to hang for treason. Very soon thereafter, Washington decided to reprieve both executions for six months. These were the first reprieves under the Constitution. In his reprieve of rebel Philip Vigol, Washington noted that "physicians" had declared Vigol "deranged in his understanding and of unsound mind."[33] For the other prisoner, Washington merely declared it "expedient" to postpone the hanging.[34] Not much of a justification. As the reprieves were set to expire, Washington pardoned both men: "the restoration of peace, order and submission to the laws . . . renders it unnecessary to make examples of those who have been convicted, the principal end of human punishment being the reformation of others."[35] This was a curious reason, for one might suppose that observers might take the lesson that unsuccessful rebels would never be punished after the restoration of peace. This might embolden future plotters and rebels. Some speculate that Washington had to pardon the two (and only) Whiskey convicts because he had received many petitions on their behalf and because their execution might stoke another uprising. If so, any candid explanation would prove troublesome. Better to say that no "examples" were necessary. Later, some of Washington's allies would rue the president's mercy.

The First Political Pardons?

Some have said that Washington's pardons were *political*.[36] They certainly were in the sense that considerations of mercy and justice played a role. But they were not political in the crass sense of disfavoring opponents, preferring co-partisans, or advancing contested policies. I do not think Washington was pursuing a political agenda other than one calculated to balance a desire for mercy against a need to encourage respect for federal law and authority. Surely, the Constitution permits, even encourages, the use of constitutional authority, via the Pardon Clause or otherwise, to inspire confidence and faith in the law.

Would specific segments of society have a greater chance of securing a pardon? Of course a nation that esteemed wealth would likely have a pardon system that favored the monied. In any society, those closest to power often secure support and relief from their government. A rich, influential, and esteemed patrician was always more likely to receive a pardon than an impoverished wretch. The Thomas Birds of the world—the foreigners, the poor, the obscure, and the uninfluential—were at a disadvantage. Again, some things never change.

The First Reasons

Washington's pardons invariably listed reasons, thereby signaling a need for *reasoned* judgment and to be seen as exercising discretion and care. As noted earlier, pardons typically were public documents, addressed to the world. All those who read them would know that *just* reasons moved Washington, often with high-sounding motives. We can learn from these stated causes.

Some grants mention a blameless mother or a family; without some form of pardon, they would be considered victims. The pardons of rebels speak of the restoration of peace and a desire to "temper . . . Justice with a reasonable extension of mercy" in appropriate cases.[37] Some pardons said that the recipient had aided law enforcement by testifying against an offender or by protecting law enforcement personnel.[38] These pardons *helped* enforce the law. One pardon claimed that the lawbreaking arose due to "certain acts of benevolence and humanity"—a situation meriting clemency.[39] One pardon reported that third parties "certified" the recipient's character to be "fair and honest," and others recalled favorable comments about the "character" of the recipient.[40] These recipients were decent fellows who inadvertently committed a crime. Washington's pardon of a ship owner mentioned the jury's recommendation of leniency and the judge's observation that the person was ignorant of the law and lacked intent to defraud the public.[41] Recall that the pardon of Samuel Dodge asserted, too, that his violation was "unintentional."[42] One pardon said the underlying acts were committed "in ignorance and misinformation" and reflected no desire to commit fraud or violate the laws.[43] Washington's pardon of a foreign consul spoke of his "respect" for the Republic of Genoa and "other good causes and considerations."[44] In one case, Washington asserted that someone had already been punished for his supposed crimes (larceny on board a vessel); he seemed to be saying that this offender had suffered enough.[45] Some pardons mentioned that, without a remission of fines and penalties, the poor soul would remain in jail indefinitely due to the practice of imprisoning those who could not pay their debts.[46] Many times, Washington would list one or two specific reasons and add that there were other "good causes" and "considerations."[47] I am sure there were.

Did Washington imagine there were unjust or illegal reasons for granting pardons? I suppose so. But there was no occasion to list *wrongful* reasons. A pardon grant would not list improper reasons for dispensing pardons. So, one cannot say for sure. How about improper reasons for *withholding* a pardon? Again, one cannot say.

What seems crystal clear is that the first president supposed there had to be *reasons* behind a grant. We can also infer that Washington believed he had to have respectable reasons to pardon, as his pardons often listed multiple reasons.

As we have seen, Washington would not pardon if he could not justify it to the "laws of [his] country," perhaps to the people of the United States.[48] That described his sense of Thomas Bird's case. One can always rationalize clemency, however. Once released from jail, a man might contribute, in many ways, to society. Washington knew this. As commander in chief, he had pardoned prisoners *indiscriminately* on days of celebration, freeing people on death row or otherwise. There was no individualized consideration, or so it seemed, on Independence Day. Perhaps he understood that an executed soldier could not fight the British. Likewise, under the new Constitution, dead or jailed prisoners could not contribute to their families, communities, or nations. Further, a pardon to someone seemingly unworthy might serve a worthy purpose—namely, strengthening the bonds between the nation and the friends and family of the recipient. That might explain the pardons of the Whiskey rebels. Washington did not pardon them because they were wonderful people; they had committed acts of violence, and he did not know them as individuals. He pardoned them to heal wounds and end an uprising.

A Stellar (First) Precedent

The first pardoner-in-chief was an astute and honorable man, always pursuing the nation's best interests as he perceived them. He was measured, cautious, thorough, inquisitive, and eager for advice. Modern presidents cannot match his level of care, because there are thousands more seeking clemency, and because our chief executives have vastly more constitutional, legal, and political responsibilities. But modern presidents could learn a thing or two by mirroring Washington's sterling example. To return to this chapter's beginnings, modern presidents ought to draw into "precedent" Washington's prudent exercise of the pardon power.[49]

* * *

Not every president's motives would be above reproach, for not every president would have Washington's record of service or his reputation for propriety. The next chapter discusses some of our nation's most infamous pardons. What links these contentious and even notorious pardons is the sense that presidents perhaps used the pardon power to advance personal interests, partisan goals, and contested policy objectives. Critics insisted that these grants of clemency were not about mercy, reconciliation, or calibration. Rather, they were said to be abuses of the pardon pen.

CHAPTER 4

Politics by Other Means

RECALL THAT WASHINGTON well knew that official conduct often could be subject to a "double interpretation."[1] He used the phrase to mean that some acts can be seen as either principled or venal. This ambiguity as to motive applied no less to acts of clemency. Why was the president forgiving a criminal or granting amnesty to a multitude? Were sound, just, and appropriate reasons motivating the clemency—concerns about innocence, mercy, calibration, reconciliation? Or was something else afoot, something nefarious?

Post-Washington, a fair number of (in)famous pardons were susceptible to multiple interpretations.[2] Detailed below are some episodes where detractors insisted or suspected that presidents pardoned for *political* or *policy* reasons. Of course, all pardons are political in the sense that presidents are elected officials and act within a political system. I mean something narrower here—specifically, the notion that certain pardons are designed wholly, or in part, to garner votes, shore up political support, secure an office, aide partisan allies, or further a divisive public policy. All the pardons discussed below were alleged to be less about calibration, innocence, and mercy, and more about advancing the interests of the president.

Obviously, these examples are not the product of random selection. I choose them because these were pardons that were controversial when issued. No one should suppose that these are the only pardons that seemed political. For instance, I say nothing about the allegation that Richard Nixon received a bribe for pardoning Jimmy Hoffa.[3] I am confident that there are other comparable stories our there. But that would only underscore my point that pardons have increasingly become an instrument of ordinary politics. While not all (or most) pardons are political, the ones that are (or are perceived as such) attract significant attention and trigger a good deal of angst.

John Adams, Rebels, and Pennsylvania

About five years after the Whiskey Rebellion, another tax rebellion brewed in Pennsylvania. In July 1798, Congress levied a tax on houses and other property. In Pennsylvania, the tax fell upon homes and land, with the value of a house determined by its number of windows. The tax aroused fierce opposition, and many refused to pay.[4]

John Fries, the son of German immigrants, organized resistance in southeastern Pennsylvania. As an itinerant auctioneer, Fries knew that many Germans opposed the tax. Fries became strident, eventually leading an armed band and forcing assessors to flee a town. Soon, a local militia company and a force of irregulars, marching to drum and fife, captured several assessors. Opposition spread to other parts of Pennsylvania. After the federal marshal began arresting people for tax resistance, rebels forcefully liberated prisoners. Alarmed, the administration of John Adams called out troops and local militia. The force marched into rebel areas and arrested insurgents. John Fries, among others, was tried for treason. He was sentenced to death.[5]

Federalists wanted Fries and others to be hanged. They had seen Shays's Rebellion (in Massachusetts), the Whiskey Rebellion, and now Fries's Rebellion, all in the space of about a decade. If Fries and his allies were not executed, they feared that America might experience a rebellion every five years. Charles Lee, the attorney general, spoke for this faction: Pennsylvania had several "bad citizens, some of whom are ignorant, refractory, headstrong, and wicked. . . . I think an exemplary punishment of rebellious conduct is more necessary and will be salutary." The former secretary of state, Timothy Pickering, claimed that two members of the Adams cabinet "were convinced that Fries ought to be executed" and that a third thought that "three of the traitors" should suffer death.[6]

Adams chose to pardon just days before the scheduled executions. The president's clemency took the form of a general amnesty for everyone involved. He waited till the end, perhaps hoping that the impending hangings might chasten the rebels and deter future malefactors. According to Adams, Fries and others were not traitors but mere rioters. They were "obscure, miserable Germans, as ignorant of our language as they were of our laws." The opposition was delighted that justice, as they saw it, was done. One even said that the executive should learn to treat "the people" with greater "delicacy" in the future.[7]

His fellow Federalists were aghast, certain that self-interest lay behind the president's amnesty. Prior to the amnesty, the party was already riven with disagreements, with Adams and Hamilton at loggerheads. Hamilton's faction was prone to see the worst in Adams. One said "I can believe Mr. Adams capable of anything to promote his personal" interests. In this case, there was a "new system of politics—the coalition" which "can alone account" for the "grace to the Jacobins" (in America, "Jacobin" was a term of abuse applied to perceived radicals). The detractor meant that Adams *was in a coalition with Jefferson.* Another Federalist went further. President Adams was seeking "to secure the office of the Vice-President under Jefferson."[8] Alexander Hamilton wrote a public letter opposing Adams, listing all his faults. He discussed the amnesty. "It was impossible to commit a greater error," said Hamilton.[9] "Every thing loudly demanded that the Executive should have acted with exemplary vigor, and should have given a striking demonstration that condign punishment would be the lot of the violent opposers of the laws."[10] The rebels should have been executed. Instead, Adams had repudiated his prior statements that were critical of Washington's Whiskey pardons and had scorned his cabinet. Adams "temporizings" were "inexplicable" causing him to lose the respect of "friends and foes."[11]

Paul Douglas Newman, an expert on the Fries Rebellion, notes that there is no evidence that Adams had conspired with Jefferson. But he says that "it is certainly likely that Adams viewed the pardon" as helpful in securing votes in Pennsylvania in the 1800 presidential contest.[12] Indeed, Adams secured far more electoral votes from Pennsylvania in 1800 than he had in 1796. Nonetheless, Adams lost the election and, of course, did not serve as Jefferson's vice president.

Was John Adams angling for votes? Some Federalists certainly thought that Adams had pardoned out of self-interest. But their claims that he wanted to form a coalition with Jefferson and serve as his vice president sound wholly absurd. Yet as Newman suggests, Adams may have known that pardons would make him more popular. But was that the motive for the pardon, the *sole* reason? Adams had others, including not being the first president to preside over hangings for treason and a stated belief that while they had committed crimes, the rebels were not guilty of *treason*. We will never know the truth of the matter. Though this was perhaps the first charge of a *base political* motive behind a pardon, this would hardly be the last.

Jefferson Pardons His Attack Dog

One contested feature of the Adams presidency was the passage and enforcement of the Sedition Act.[13] The controversial and notorious Act made it a crime to publish false, scandalous, and malicious writings against the government. The Act's opponents said it transgressed the Constitution. Federalists argued otherwise, claiming it protected the government from unwarranted and debilitating attacks. After its passage, the Administration made it a practice to read the newspapers and send seditious writings to the US attorneys, ordering them to prosecute.[14] Some Republicans were in jail because of the zeal of the prosecutors.[15]

Thomas Jefferson thought the Sedition Act was a constitutional abomination. Once he entered office, he treated the Sedition Act as a "nullity."[16] He pardoned two people prosecuted under the Act, including newsman James Callender.[17] Callender was no stranger to Jefferson, for Jefferson had long patronized Callendar's caustic attacks on the Federalists, sending funds periodically. Callender's pardon would prove remarkably vexing and lead to a split between Callendar and his former sponsor.

First, Callender sought the return of a $200 fine stemming from his conviction. The question was whether the president's pardon could be the basis for refunding it. According to a US marshal, the president could not return the fine because it was now in the Treasury, and, per the Constitution, only Congress could authorize its withdrawal from the Treasury.[18] This dispute took months to sort out, infuriating Callender.[19] The attorney general eventually concluded that if the remission occurred before the money had been deposited into the Treasury, the fine should be returned to Callender.[20] In other words, though the government held the money, the funds might not be "in" the Treasury. Callender got his money.[21] But critics protested that the government had unconstitutionally raided the Treasury to fund a political ally.[22] The critics supposed that the fine was in the Treasury the moment the marshal received it and hence Jefferson could not remit the fine.

Second, Callender grew ornery. The delay in returning the fine had annoyed him. But Callender became white-hot after Jefferson refused to appoint him as a postmaster. Because Callender had long served Jefferson and the Democratic-Republican cause, he thought he deserved the patronage. Jefferson thought otherwise, leading an irate Callender to target his former patron. Callender took up his pen and attacked Jefferson with an unrelenting fury. First, Callender disclosed that Jefferson had long subsidized his attacks on Washington and other Federalists. This was shocking enough. Second, Callender also unearthed a scandal—that Jefferson had fathered children with Sally Hemings. As Professor Annette Gordon-Reed points out, Callender had traveled to Monticello to verify whether long-standing rumors were true. Callender called Hemings a "concubine" and otherwise abused Hemings, likely because he was a racist. Finally, Callender recounted Jefferson's supposed attempt to have an affair with a married neighbor. These revelations must have vexed Jefferson. Callender died in 1803.[23]

The news that Jefferson had long bankrolled Callender understandably colored how people perceived the pardon. Callender had penned stinging rebukes of Washington. He had exposed Hamilton's affair with Maria Reynolds and had accused the secretary of financial improprieties.[24] In 1800, Callender had excoriated the supposedly corrupt administration of John Adams. So, Jefferson had been underwriting attacks on Washington, Hamilton, and Adams. Given his patronage of Callender, the pardon appeared to some as an abuse of the pardon pen, a reward to a longtime ally.

In 1804, Abigail Adams made this exact assertion. She claimed that Jefferson had pardoned Callender precisely because Callender had sharply attacked Jefferson's political opponents. She wrote a letter to Jefferson complaining that he had liberated "a wretch who was suffering the just punishment of the Law due to his . . . basest libel, the lowest and vilest slander, which malice could invent" against John Adams.[25] Jefferson responded that his longtime monetary support for Callender had nothing to do with Callender's calumnies of Adams.[26] Rather, the money was intended as aid to a "genius," said Jefferson. "My charities to [Callender] were no more meant as encouragement for his scurrilities than those I give to the beggar at my door are meant as a reward for the vices of his life." In fact, "no body sooner disapproved of his writings than I did, or wished more that he be silent." This was, of course, utterly silly.

What of the pardon for Callendar? Jefferson declared that he had:

> discharged every person under punishment . . . because I considered . . . [the Sedition Act] to be [an unconstitutional] nul-

lity as absolute and as palpable as if Congress had ordered us to fall down and worship a golden image. . . . It was accordingly done in every instance, without asking what the offenders had done, or against whom they had offended, but whether the pains they were suffering were inflicted under the pretended Sedition law.[27]

Abigail Adams was unyielding. She tartly noted that neither she nor anyone else she knew viewed the pardon as grounded on constitutional principle.[28] Jefferson had pardoned his ally, an attack dog. That the hound later bit its former benefactor did nothing to allay her deep suspicions.

Jefferson had pardoned two people under an act that he said was unconstitutional. Posterity agrees with his assessment, as moderns generally consider the Sedition Act unconstitutional. But at the time, the Federalists thought the Act was constitutional. And the beneficiaries of Jefferson's pardons were political allies, one of whom he had long subsidized. Were Jefferson's motives pure, base, or something in the middle? We cannot say for certain. However, as in the case of John Adams and his pardons in the wake of the Fries's Rebellion, observers were utterly convinced that Jefferson had wielded the pardon pen as a political tool, this time to reward an ally who had lacerated Jefferson's opponents for years.

Abraham Lincoln's Conditional Amnesty

Today, Abraham Lincoln is beloved by all. But even saints have their critics and sometimes those detractors have a point or two. Here we examine Lincoln's amnesty for Confederates. Many Northerners opposed it on the grounds that it coddled traitors; after all, it sought to forgive their perfidious treason.[29] But it also had an additional element, one designed to protect the Emancipation Proclamation.[30] Although we rightly celebrate that Proclamation, Lincoln's amnesty offer advanced his policy and moral agendas, both of which were contested at the time. Lincoln's amnesty raises the delicate question: Does the Constitution authorize the president to make a pardon conditional on support for contested presidential policies?

In 1862, Congress's Confiscation Act authorized the president to issue amnesties.[31] This was legally superfluous because the Constitution had already done the same.[32] In 1863, the president issued an amnesty, citing the Act *and* the Constitution.[33] With a number of exceptions including one related to Confederate officers, civil and military, the Proclamation of Amnesty and Reconstruction extended to "all persons who have . . . participated in the existing rebellion." It came "with [a] restoration of all rights of property, except as to slaves, and . . . upon the condition that every such person shall take . . . an oath." The oath had this form:

> I,___ ___, do solemnly swear, in presence of Almighty God, that I will henceforth faithfully support, protect, and defend the Constitution of the United States and the Union of the States thereunder; and that I will, in like manner, abide by and faithfully support all acts of congress passed during the existing rebellion with reference to slaves, so long and so far as not repealed, modified, or held void by congress, or by decision of the supreme court; and that I will, in like manner, abide by and faithfully support all proclamations of the President made during the existing rebellion having reference to slaves, so long and so far as not modified or declared void by decision of the supreme court. So help me God.[34]

Oath takers pledged to "abide by and faithfully support" all congressional laws and presidential proclamations related to slavery, the most prominent of which was the Emancipation Proclamation. At a minimum, this meant that they had to honor these acts and proclamations, meaning they had to conform their behavior to them. This was provocative enough because some thought one or both were unconstitutional. What else did the oath entail? Could the oath takers protest these laws and edicts? I doubt it, for they would be undermining, and not supporting, these laws and edicts. Could they sue to overturn slave confiscations on the grounds that they were unconstitutional? Again, I do not see how. Could oath takers vote for candidates who hoped to overturn these acts and proclamations? Perhaps not. The president offered amnesty to Confederates if they laid down their arms *and* backed congressional laws and presidential edicts that had stoked legitimate controversies.

One Southerner rejected the demand to oppose slavery as "strange and absurd," and another complained that the amnesty was stingier than those offered by "Christian Princes." Northern reactions varied. Critics said it was a "Despot's Edict, a ukase from the chambers of an autocrat" and "a device to perpetuate the effect of the abolition measures in the Southern States." Some papers said it was an election ploy, meant to secure his renomination.[35]

Lincoln's moral stance on slavery was undoubtedly right. "If slavery is not wrong, nothing is wrong."[36] But there is the nagging question of whether a president may condition a pardon on political support for contested policies, even in times of crisis. This was not merely a demand that rebels follow the constitutional laws of Congress. Of course, a president can condition a pardon on future compliance with all constitutional laws. Nor was it even a demand to follow the laws of Congress, whether constitutional or not. Lincoln purchased loyalty and submission to *his* policy preferences, some of which might have been unconstitutional. Vow to honor and support my edicts, he demanded.

Imagine a modern president making this promise to a celebrity: "Your enormous tax penalty is pardoned, and you will be released from prison immediately, but only if you publicly pledge support for my Medicare reforms." Or imagine a president presenting a big city mayor with the following proposition: "I will pardon your crimes if you support my deportation policies." Many people, including a district court, believed it was inappropriate for President Donald Trump to make a similar offer to New York Mayor Eric Adams.[37] But one might suppose that Lincoln made a similar offer first, to thousands of Southerners. To be sure, Lincoln made his offer in a time of crisis; yet one might suppose that the breadth of the power to attach conditions to pardons does not turn on whether the country is in an emergency.

To be clear, I am not saying that what Lincoln did was wrong, constitutionally or otherwise. Rather, I merely point out that what he did was controversial at the time, and that the limits on the power to issue conditional pardons remains contested. While everyone understands that the president has the power to place conditions on a pardon, either requiring preceding action or subsequent conduct (or both), many suppose that there must be some limits to the sorts of conditions that the president may impose.[38] Could the president grant a pardon on condition of a campaign donation? I hope not. Could the president grant a pardon conditioned on a man accepting Christ as his savior? Again, I think not. Could a pardon be conditioned on a vote? I trust not. But the power to issue conditional pardons raises these sorts of perplexing questions.

Andrew Johnson's Generous Amnesties

With the wretched assassination of Lincoln, Andrew Johnson took over. He was a unionist with southern sympathies. "I love the Southern people . . . and [will] do all in my power to restore them to the state of happiness and prosperity which they formerly enjoyed." In May of 1865, he granted an amnesty, one that similarly turned on "abid[ing] by and faithfully support[ing] all [slavery] laws and proclamations" made during the rebellion.[39] Rebels with over $20,000 in taxable property were excluded, meaning that plantation owners were omitted. The number of exceptions heartened those who favored tough measures for the rebels. But, like Lincoln, Johnson freely handed out individual pardons, even to those left out of the proclamation. So, the exceptions were sometimes more apparent than real.[40]

Tensions between Johnson and the Radical Republicans in Congress boiled over. The Radicals sought to reconstruct the South and bring the former rebels to heel. In 1867, Congress repealed the statutory authority to grant amnesties, leaving the president to act on his constitutional authority alone. Some members of Congress denied that the president could issue amnesties. Senators were particularly worried that pardons would restore forfeited property to the wealthy rebels at the forefront of the rebellion. Some of these Senators supposed that pardons could not restore property, and that only Congress could authorize property restoration.[41]

That same year, Johnson issued a more generous second amnesty, eliminating many of the exceptions. This time, there were only three exclusions: Confederate officers, those who mistreated Union prisoners, and those in military or civil confinement.[42] The exceptions were so narrow that only three hundred Confederates were excluded.[43]

The criticism was swift and furious. Johnson was obstructing Reconstruction, said opponents. "The animus of the proclamation . . . is an effort to impede reconstruction to throw the control of the Southern States more fully into the hands of the rebels." His second proclamation was "Executive usurpation [little] short of dictatorship" and designed to defy Congress. Every Southern state would be a "paradise" for "traitors." It was an "outrage and insult to our loyal dead," and the "drunkard"—Johnson—ought to be impeached. It was "the greatest rebel victory since Bull Run." Others saw the amnesty as a precursor to another rebellion or a coup. Johnson would combat Congress with a Southern army. A new Northern army, one not controlled by the Commander in Chief, would have to take the field to thwart the sitting president. Of course, not all were critical, for the South and its Northern sympathizers were elated: "All honor to the statesmen who have proved themselves

President . . . of the whole people."[44] Southerners should register to vote and then vote for Jackson, some said.

The House impeached the president for offenses unrelated to the pardon, and the conviction failed in the Senate by one vote. After surviving that scare, Johnson issued his third amnesty, excluding only those already subject to criminal prosecution for treason.[45] All those amnestied would receive their forfeited property, except property "legally divested under the laws."[46] Slaves had been legally divested by the Thirteenth Amendment, the one that barred slavery. The third amnesty was issued on the very day that Democrats met in New York to nominate a candidate. Further, a letter supposedly from the president appeared in the New York press saying that he favored a "universal amnesty."[47] Though Johnson received many votes, he did not secure the nomination. Yet the Democrats did endorse a "universal amnesty."

In December 1868, Johnson issued a fourth amnesty, a Christmas-day amnesty. It pardoned *every remaining rebel,* including Jefferson Davis, Robert E. Lee, and a few others left unpardoned in the third amnesty.[48] Johnson said that a universal amnesty would

> tend to secure permanent peace, order, and prosperity throughout the land, and to renew and fully restore confidence and fraternal feeling among the whole people, and their respect for and attachment to the National Government, designed by its patriotic founders for the general good.[49]

No other amnesties would follow because there was no one left to pardon for rebellion.

Members of Congress were up in arms. Senators sought a copy of the amnesty and the legal authority for it. Johnson cited the Constitution and the amnesty precedents of Washington, Adams, and Lincoln. The Senate Judiciary Committee issued a report denying that the president could issue amnesties, saying that pardon and amnesty were not synonymous.[50] But nothing came of the report, and subsequent presidents have continued to issue amnesties.

Perhaps reconciliation motivated the amnesties. Alternatively, they might have reflected a deep and abiding empathy for the South. Finally, a desire to secure the Democratic nomination for the presidency might have played a role. Was the third amnesty an electoral gambit, one designed to secure convention votes?

I think so, at least in part. The first two amnesties preceded the Democratic Convention and the third was timed to coincide with it. According to Paul Bergeron, in June 1868 "Johnson and his cabinet took a bold step to promote his candidacy by developing a new amnesty proclamation." One of his supporters in New York wrote to urge Johnson to issue the proclamation soon, assuring him that "you will make large capital" thereby.[51] On July 4, he issued the amnesty, timed to coincide with Independence Day and the onset of the Democratic Convention, held in New York. He was told by a friend that the Third Amnesty "was beneficial in the extreme" amongst convention delegates.[52] Finally, remember that Johnson apparently said that he would grant a general, unconditional amnesty, something the Convention sought.

Johnson failed to secure the nomination. But an unsuccessful gambit should not obscure the political machination: he had exploited the pardon pen to advance his political interests. As we shall see, other presidents have pursued the same strategy.

Ford Pardons Nixon

There were, of course, pardon controversies between 1868 and 1974. But we will leap to President Richard Nixon and Vice President Gerald Ford. Nixon had been implicated in the Watergate conspiracy. He confronted a House impeachment, a Senate trial and removal, and a possible criminal trial.

Nixon confronted bad options. He was told that he could not pardon himself. But perhaps *President* Ford would do that. Indeed,

White House insiders sought Vice President Ford's opinions on what the president ought to do and asked whether *President* Ford would pardon Nixon. Ford declined to offer any assurances. He understood the terms of the "deal" on offer. He had refused that deal.[53]

Nixon resigned soon thereafter. Congress dropped impeachment, but criminal prosecution still loomed as a possibility. On September 8, 1974, about a month after Nixon's resignation, President Ford granted Nixon a "full, free, and absolute pardon." The pardon listed reasons: A trial might not begin for a year or more, during which the nation's harmony "could be irreparably lost." Further, a trial "will cause prolonged and divisive debate over the propriety of exposing to further punishment and degradation a man who has already paid the unprecedented penalty of relinquishing the highest elective office of the United States."[54]

Ford also made prepared remarks. He believed in equal justice, he said, but also that the law respected "reality." The reality, as Ford saw it, was that Nixon might not receive equal justice but would be "cruelly and excessively punished" by a long and potentially inconclusive trial, one that might violate "due process." Further, the nation's psyche concerned him. Ford could not "prolong the bad dreams" that plagued one and all. He had the constitutional authority to "firmly shut and seal this book," and it was his duty to ensure "domestic tranquility." He then mentioned angels, God, and that Nixon would continue to suffer even after the pardon.[55] I doubt that any president has ever offered *more* reasons for a pardon.

Critics beheld a corrupt bargain with the pardon issued in exchange for Nixon's resignation.[56] The *Washington Post* said the pardon was "nothing less than a continuation of the cover-up."[57] "We don't even know what acts by Mr. Nixon the President is pardoning, because, all the facts and all the evidence are not yet available," said Senator Walter Mondale.[58] Further, we "may never know the full dimensions of Mr. Nixon's complicity in the worst political scandal in American history," Mondale said.[59] *The New*

York Times called the Nixon pardon a "profoundly unwise, divisive, and unjust act" that had destroyed the new president's "credibility as a man of judgment, candor, and competence."[60]

Whispers of corruption led President Ford to testify before the House Judiciary Committee. His approval rating plunged from 71 percent to 50 percent.[61] Ford eventually lost the 1976 election to Jimmy Carter. But years later, former critics came around. In 2001, Ford received a "Profile in Courage" award. At the presentation, Senator Ted Kennedy described how he went from a critic to someone who saw Ford as courageous.[62]

In his book on the Ford pardon, Jeffrey Toobin argues that the pardon was a "terrible decision," but that Ford acted honorably and with admirable candor.[63] I am inclined to think the decision was brave. But of course, I cannot peer into Ford's heart and divine his true purposes. What is clear is that, once again, many insisted that the clemency rested on ignoble motivations.

George H. W. Bush Pardons Political Allies

Although Reagan won on a campaign of "morning in America," much of his second term was a nightmare, consumed with the Iran-Contra scandal. The executive covertly sold arms to Iran to secure the return of American hostages. The proceeds of the sales went to the Contras in El Salvador, an armed resistance to the left-wing Sandinista government. Congress had authorized neither the arms sales nor the Contra funding.

The investigation of the scandal spanned the Reagan, Bush, and Clinton presidencies. On Christmas Eve, 1992, President George W. Bush pardoned several Iran-Contra figures, including Caspar Weinberger, the former secretary of defense.[64] Lawrence Walsh, the Independent Counsel investigating Iran-Contra, was incensed. Bush's pardon meant that "the Iran-contra coverup, which has continued for more than six years, has now been completed."[65] Weinberger was about to face prosecution. A trial "would have exposed new evidence of the Administration's efforts to conceal the facts of the Iran arms sales from the public and from Congress."[66] It may also have forced Bush to testify at trial, as a defense witness. Walsh declared that Bush was a "target" and that the president had engaged in "misconduct" by failing to hand over his diary.[67] Bush may have "illegally withheld documents" from investigators.[68]

Walsh concluded his work in the fall of 1993, never bringing any charges against Bush, either for his acts as vice president or his acts as president. To Bush's defenders, Walsh had been a rogue prosecutor, expending millions on a quixotic hunt, a modern-day Captain Ahab. For Bush's detractors, the pardons must have validated fears voiced at the Founding. Recall that some Anti-Federalists claimed that a president might pardon allies to hide his perfidy. To these critics, the Anti-Federalists had been vindicated, with woeful consequences for the truth. Were Walsh and the Bush detractors right? This is hardly the place to litigate the underlying scandal and Bush's role in it. Count it as another example of widespread suspicions that the pardon pen was wielded to further the narrow interests of the incumbent. To some, Bush had all but pardoned himself.

Bill Clinton Pardons Political Allies

In 1999, Hillary Clinton formed an exploratory committee to run for the Senate in 2000.[69] Puerto Rican support in the primary and general elections in New York would prove crucial.[70] In August 1999, her husband, President Bill Clinton, commuted the sentences of sixteen members of FALN, a Puerto Rican group that had set off over a hundred bombs in the United States.[71] The sixteen were serving sentences from thirty-five to one hundred and five years. Some people, including members of Congress, had long sought a pardon for members of the FALN. But clemency had long been opposed by US attorneys, the FBI, and victims of FALN.[72]

Hillary Clinton's campaign said she "supported" the commutations of those FALN who renounced violence.[73] But amidst a firestorm, she retreated and withdrew her support three days later.[74] Remarkably, Congress condemned the clemency, 95–2 in the Senate and 311–41 in the House.[75] The House investigated, but Clinton refused to hand over documents and barred official testimony.[76]

Soon, another controversy arose—"Pardongate." Clinton issued 140 pardons on his last day of office, January 20, 2001.[77] Among those pardoned were Clinton's half-brother, Clinton's former business partner, Democratic politicians, and more terrorists. But two pardons were perhaps especially political. First was the pardoning of Hasidim—orthodox Jews. Some Hasidim had defrauded the federal government by crafting a fictitious school to receive federal funding. In 2000, in supposed anticipation of a pardon, the sect's leader endorsed Clinton. In other words, the alleged deal was that the Hasidim would vote en masse for Hillary Clinton and expected a clemency from President Clinton after the Senate election.[78]

Second was the last-minute pardon of Marc Rich, a fugitive from justice. Rich owed $48 million in taxes and was charged with fifty-one counts.[79] He fled to Switzerland during the trial. Per his commutation from the president, Rich had to pay a $1 million fine and waive use of the pardon in any civil proceeding. Critics complained that Denise Rich, his former wife, had made substantial donations to the expected William Clinton Presidential Library and to Hillary Clinton's campaign.[80]

Again, some saw a quid pro quo. Others made the less charged accusation that the contributions influenced Clinton's decision to commute. "To my mind, there can be no justification for pardoning a fugitive from justice," said the senior New York Senator, Chuck Schumer; the pardon "stands our justice system on its head and makes a mockery of it." Senator Dick Durbin said the pardon "certainly raises the appearance of impropriety."[81]

Both chambers of Congress commenced investigations. Were the pardons unlawful, and was the president's half-brother involved in a scheme to sell pardons? The US attorney for the Southern

District of New York investigated all of Clinton's last-minute acts of clemency.

No criminal charges were brought. But these grants of clemency injured Clinton's reputation. "It was contemptuous," said Senator Patrick J. Leahy, Democrat from Vermont. "It was inexcusable."[82] President Jimmy Carter came to the same conclusion: "I don't think there is any doubt that some of the factors in his pardon were attributable to his large gifts. In my opinion, that was disgraceful."[83] Former President Clinton denied this, of course. But his rebuttal did little to convince his many critics.

* * *

Throughout our history, when it came to some of the most (in)famous pardons, observers have wrestled with the problem of "double interpretation." They often sensed that the pardons were (or might have been) grounded in political calculations of some sort. In his 1804 letter to Abigail Adams, Jefferson acknowledged the issue and the difficulties of discerning motives. Jefferson wrote, "it was certainly possible that my motives for contributing to the relief of Callender . . . might have been to protect, encourage and reward slander."[84] This is utterly remarkable, even as it states the obvious. But he went on to muse that his motives "may also have been those which inspire ordinary charities to objects of distress, meritorious or not, or the obligations of an oath to protect the constitution, violated by an unauthorised act of Congress." Jefferson's defense was to supply two other motives—both of which would have been perfectly fine reasons.

Indeed, every president accused of wrongful motives can always invoke sound ones, for there are so many from which to choose: rehabilitation, calibration, mercy, and so on. "Which of these were my motives must be decided by a regard to the general tenor of my life," wrote Jefferson. He would, and he was "not afraid to appeal to the nation at large, to posterity, and . . . to that being who sees himself our motives, who will judge us from his own knolege of them."[85] Posterity is still wondering both what his motives were and what impulses drove his successors as they made equally controversial, politically inflected pardons. Was it mercy, calibration, or a crass political maneuver?

Although this chapter ends with the Clinton pardons, they would hardly be the last to raise the specter of whether clemency served to secure political support. The new millennium brought new controversies to the fore about the optics of aiding political allies and rewarding donors. With the Trump and Biden administrations, the concerns and the controversies multiplied. Today, pardons seem almost entirely a matter of politics. That's not quite true. Yet we do seem to be in a brave new pardon world, and one must doubt whether a return to the status quo ante is in the offing. Any vestige of naïveté is gone and cynicism, born of hard experience, grips our minds. Almost every pardon looks political, in the sense that many of us harbor suspicions that they have little or nothing to do with mercy but are instead about the continuation of politics by other means.

CHAPTER 5

A Tale of Two Clemencies

BILL CLINTON'S immediate successors, George W. Bush and Barack Obama, were perhaps intent on steering clear of pardon storms, and avoiding any hint that pardons might be grounded on crass political calculations. They saw Clinton's mess—the awful optics, the heated congressional hearings, the bipartisan denunciations—and erred on the side of caution. In one case, Bush (seemingly) pardoned a man and immediately backtracked.[1] His reason? Critics, and ordinary Americans, might regard the pardon as payback for campaign contributions, the very sort of conjecture that plagued Clinton's pardon of Marc Rich.[2] (More on Bush's reversal in Chapter 6.) Bush and Obama knew their reputations would not suffer from rejecting most pardon applicants. Yet the aversion declined over time, and supposed lessons were forgotten, leading President Obama's successors to be more adventurous and aggressive. Exploiting the pardon pen for political or personal purposes was perhaps too tempting, bordering on irresistible.

In his first term, President Trump pardoned his daughter's father-in-law, Charles Kushner.[3] He pardoned Maricopa County Sheriff Joe Arpaio.[4] And he granted clemency to friends and aides entangled in Robert Mueller's Russian influence investigation, including Michael Flynn, Roger Stone, and Paul Manafort.[5]

But nothing Trump did in his first term could approach the bizarre and lurid confluence of clemency on the eve of the Inauguration and Inauguration Day, 2025. Indeed, in the annals of pardon history, nothing before comes close to what transpired on January 19 and 20, 2025.

Per the Twentieth Amendment, presidential terms begin (and end) at noon on January 20, every four years.[6] That makes Inauguration Day the only day that we have two presidents the outgoing president serving until noon and the newly inaugurated serving thereafter. On January 19, 2025, President Biden pardoned several members of his family.[7] The family pardons were preemptive pardons, issued in advance of any prosecution or conviction. Further they were blanket pardons that encompassed any nonviolent crimes the recipients might have committed in the previous decade.[8] This was on the heels of Biden's even broader pardon of his son, Hunter Biden, which covered the same ten-year span but also included violent offenses.[9] Further, the president preemptively pardoned the members and staff of the House committee that had investigated the events of January 6, 2021, along with Capitol Police officers who had testified before that committee.[10] Print newspapers announced the controversial decisions on the morning of January 20, and highlighted denunciations from both sides of the political aisle.[11]

Trump entered office at noon and followed suit. He signed an amnesty for those who had stormed the Capitol four years earlier.[12] During the 2024 campaign for the presidency, Trump had insisted that the hundreds incarcerated for January 6 crimes were "hostages."[13] This signaled that they were political prisoners of a sort, targeted due to their devotion to him. He redeemed his promise to free the "hostages," not making any exceptions even for violent offenders.[14] The January 20 pardon was so far-reaching (and so poorly worded) that its scope would be the subject of considerable disputes in the courts.

This chapter considers the extraordinary clemency of January 19 and 20, arguing that both grants were partly grounded in partisan considerations, most prominently a profound distrust of the opposing administration. After Trump's first term, prosecutors brought charges against him in various jurisdictions. A few Democrats conceded that state prosecutors had targeted Trump.[15] "It's a coincidence that [Manhattan District Attorney Alvin] Bragg goes after Trump and [New York Attorney General] Tish James goes after Trump and Georgia goes after Trump. That's all a coincidence," Andrew Cuomo scoffed. "It feeds the cynicism, and that's the cancer in our body politic right now."[16] Cuomo was all but saying that these three prosecutions were motivated by politics.

Throughout the 2024 campaign, Trump had promised retribution. As his inauguration approached, Democrats were skittish and fearful, certain that the incoming administration would weaponize prosecutions. For some of these Democrats, pardons were absolutely necessary to preclude Trumpian revenge. Biden evidently agreed. Meanwhile, Trump and his allies were utterly certain that Democrats had already weaponized the justice system against him and his supporters. Why shouldn't a reinstalled Trump wield the pardon pen to undo all those partisan prosecutions?

Biden's Midnight Pardons

There are two stories behind Biden's midnight pardons. The first story relates to a genuine fear that the incoming president, Donald Trump, might prosecute his political opponents. As a candidate for a second term, Trump had told his supporters, "I am your retribution."[17] The Republican candidate had a long list of grievances. According to Trump, General Mark Milley's phone call to Chinese officials, making representations and assurances to them that the president had not authorized, was "an act so egregious that, in times gone by, the punishment would have been DEATH."[18] Trump also declared that members of the January 6 House Committee should be imprisoned for their alleged destruction of evidence: "For what they did, honestly, they *should* go to jail."[19] While Trump never threatened prosecution of Anthony Fauci, the former director of the National Institute of Allergy and Infectious Diseases, his supporters voiced strong support for it. "My pronouns are Prosecute / Fauci," Elon Musk tweeted in 2022.[20] Texas Senator Ted Cruz insisted that

"Dr. Fauci flat-out lied to Congress"—a federal offense.[21] Given the sentiments coming from the president-elect and his allies, many supposed that the new Trump administration would prosecute Milley, Fauci, and the January 6 Committee.[22]

Biden blocked that. On January 19, 2025, Biden preemptively pardoned Milley, Fauci, and the January 6 Committee.[23] The clemency encompassed some of their official actions, not their personal lives. Incoming President Trump would be barred from prosecuting them for the pardoned offenses. Many who received the pardons must have been greatly relieved. They would not face the extreme anxiety that accompanies a criminal investigation and prosecution, and they would dodge the feared retribution. Though contentious enough, these were the less divisive of Biden's midnight pardons.

The second tale was more scandalous. For many years, Joseph Biden had been involved in a sordid business, where *he* was the product. His family had been charging for access, perceived or real, to Joseph Biden.[24] Biden had an "all-in-the family approach to business and politicking," as *Politico's* Ben Schreckinger phrased it, "that dates back a half-century to the president's first Senate bid, run primarily by his parents and siblings."[25] While he was vice president, Biden took his son, Hunter, on official trips overseas.[26] He met with Hunter's business associates at the Naval Observatory, the vice president's official residence.[27] For Joseph Biden, family came first, with his son Hunter and his brother James Biden the most prominent beneficiaries.[28] But other family members received funds, too, from the schemes.[29]

Speaking of his business relationships, Hunter Biden admitted in 2011 that they had "nothing to do with me . . . and everything to do with my last name."[30] He and his business partner supplied "vice-presidential cuff links . . . to friends, associates or prospective clients."[31] "They secured tickets to White House events, including dinners, holiday parties and the annual Easter Egg Roll . . . strategizing over which business associates should receive them."[32]

During the Biden administration, the Department of Justice investigated Hunter Biden and his uncle James Biden.[33] Hunter was prosecuted and convicted.[34] With the threat of further investigations and prosecutions looming, Biden staved off both with lame-duck pardons.

The first, in December 2024, covered his son.[35] During the Biden presidency, Hunter Biden had been convicted on gun charges and had pled guilty to nine tax-related charges, including three felonies.[36] For months, Biden had insisted that he would not pardon his son.[37] "I said I'd abide by the jury['s] decision, and I will do that," the president declared. "And I will not pardon him."[38] But after the 2024 presidential election, the awful optics of pardoning his son (and breaking his promise) no longer mattered, and Biden rescued the ensnared Hunter. At that point, nothing that Biden did would sway an election. The new reality made the decision obvious, if it was not manifest before. A politician who had long aided his son's schemes was not a president who would abandon his son, leaving him to rot in jail.

Hunter's December 1 clemency was a stunning *blanket* pardon: Hunter was pardoned for any "offenses against the United States which he has committed or may have committed or taken part in during the period from January 1, 2014 through December 1, 2024."[39] In other words, the pardon encompassed *any and all offenses* that Hunter might have committed across that ten-year period. To some critics, this deliberate wording suggested not only tax evasion and gun crimes, but perhaps other crimes.[40] Margaret Love, a former official in the Justice Department, said she had "never seen language like this in a pardon document that purports to pardon offenses that have not apparently even been charged, with the exception of the Nixon pardon."[41] Even compared to the Nixon pardon, Hunter's covered a longer period.[42]

Anticipating the firestorm, Biden supplied reasons. The son who long had profited from the family name was now suffering because of it. "Hunter was singled out only because he is my son—and that is wrong," the President continued, claiming that "raw politics has infected this process and it led to a miscarriage of justice." It had to stop: "Enough is enough." Biden hoped that Americans "will understand why a father and a President would come to this decision."[43]

Pardoning Hunter before the election would have forced the Democratic nominee, Kamala Harris, to navigate a minefield of awkward questions. Harris would have had to deflect, endorse the pardon, or denounce it. The blanket pardon for Hunter would have thrown her off balance for days, if not weeks. But if that explains why the pardon was delayed, then why did it happen on December 1, rather than right before Biden left office? One can only speculate, but the timing of the actual pardon seemed related to the fact that Hunter was scheduled to be sentenced in mid-December for his gun crime and tax evasion convictions. The president perhaps sought to avoid the humiliation of two public sentencings of his son.[44] If it weren't for those pending sentencings, the president likely would have waited until the last day of his term to pardon Hunter in conjunction with the other relatives.

On January 19, 2025, President Biden pardoned his brother Francis Biden; his brother James Biden and his wife, Sara; and his sister, Valerie, and her husband, John Owens.[45] This clemency was blanket, as well, encompassing multiple types of offenses and covering a slightly longer period.[46] But these family pardons excluded *violent* offenses, marking a contrast with the more sweeping pardon for Hunter.[47] Again, the president issued a justification: "My family has been subjected to unrelenting attacks and threats, motivated solely by a desire to hurt me—the worst kind of partisan politics. . . . [B]aseless and politically motivated investigations wreak havoc on the lives, safety, and financial security of targeted individuals and their families."[48] Conscious that many people would assume only the guilty needed a pardon, Biden emphasized that was not the case: "The issuance of these pardons should not be mistaken as an acknowledgment that they engaged in any wrongdoing, nor should acceptance be misconstrued as an admission of guilt for any offense."[49] He was right, of course. But many still drew that exact conclusion.[50] Indeed, as noted, James Biden was the subject of a criminal investigation by federal prosecutors.[51] So, as much as Democrats might have feared Trumpian reprisals, this was not only about Trump and his campaign for retribution.

Republican reaction to these family pardons was mostly critical. Little surprise there. One representative said that Biden "will go down as one of the most corrupt presidents in American history."[52] Yet there was some surprising commentary. "Most Americans can sympathize with a father's decision to pardon his son," another Republican observed, "even if they disagree."[53] Democrats were dismayed. "This is a bad precedent that could be abused by later Presidents and will sadly tarnish his reputation," said one.[54] Of the family pardons, one senator said that Biden had "dangerously expanded the use of pardons in a way that could be unfortunate in the future."[55] Colorado Senator Michael Bennet said Biden's pardon of his son placed "personal interest ahead of duty and further erodes Americans' faith that the justice system is fair and equal for all."[56]

Trump's Amnesty

For weeks after the 2020 election, President Donald Trump insisted that he had won the election and that the other side had cheated.[57] Per Trump there were lost votes, ballot harvestings, and other shenanigans, dirty tricks that enabled Joe Biden to secure an electoral college majority.[58] Still, the electors voted in their states and collectively signaled that Biden had won.[59]

But Trump wanted states and federal actors to delay the electoral count to be held in Congress on January 6. Where Biden won a state's electoral votes, Trump wanted the state to send a Trump slate of electors. This might obscure, or cast into doubt, who won that state's electoral votes, or so Trump hoped. Furthermore, Trump pressed Vice President Mike Pence to disallow some electoral votes or to send the votes back to the states for reconsideration of the popular vote tallies.[60] Trump had lost, so delay, wild accusations, and chaos would be a strategy.

Those stratagems proved ineffective, as by January 6, Trump knew that neither the vice president nor his party allies in Congress would block the electoral count. That morning, the president spoke to some 53,000 people gathered for a rally at the Ellipse, an area south of the White House. In comments lasting over an hour, he asserted that Big Tech had rigged the election by suppressing news stories that favored Republicans, denied that Joseph Biden received eighty million real votes (just "eighty million computer votes"), and complained of an election "stolen by emboldened radical-left Democrats . . . and stolen by the fake news media." At the outset, he assured the crowd, "We will stop the steal." Near the end, he appealed to the patriotism his supporters shared: "We have over-whelming pride in this great country and we have it deep in our souls. Together, we are determined to defend and preserve govern-ment of the people, by the people and for the people. . . . And we fight. We fight like hell. And if you don't fight like hell, you're not going to have a country anymore." Finally, he encouraged the crowd to walk down Pennsylvania Avenue and try to give the Republicans at the Capitol "the kind of pride and boldness that they need to take back our country."[61]

By the time the throng had reached the Capitol, Trump was back at the White House.[62] Apparently, the president would fight like hell from the cushy confines of the West Wing. Protestors broke into the Capitol, occupying it for hours.[63] Although the typical demonstrator bore no intent to harm anyone, members of Congress justifiably worried that some were there to cause mayhem and violence. And there were acts of violence that day.[64]

Defenders of the president have emphasized that, in his remarks, he stated: "I know that everyone here will soon be marching over to the Capitol building to peacefully and patriotically make your voices heard."[65] The president was utterly reckless, however, and bears some responsibility for the riot. Not only that day but for weeks the president had been saying that the election was rigged and stolen. For a crowd already aggrieved, an explicit reminder of the need to "fight like hell" would have felt like an exhortation.[66] In that context, the remark about a peaceful march was too anemic. His speech was akin to lighting a match near an open gas tank and simultaneously blowing air on that match. Sometimes, blowing on a flame only stokes it.

AFTER TRUMP LEFT OFFICE, individuals who stormed the Capitol were charged with crimes including trespassing, disorderly conduct, unlawful entry, assaulting or impeding law enforcement officers, and seditious conspiracy.[67] By January 2025, more than fifteen hundred people had been charged with crimes, and over eleven hundred had been convicted.[68]

President Trump could have pardoned the Capitol rioters during his first term; after all, he was still president for about two weeks after January 6. Such pardons would have been divisive—extremely so—but potential controversy had not stopped lame-duck presidents in the past. For that matter, Trump had issued other divisive lame-duck pardons.[69] Lame ducks are optimally situated to make unpopular decisions, because they suffer no electoral consequences. Relatedly, lame-duck pardons do not jeopardize anything of substance, because presidents have no legislative initiatives as they are almost out the door. A lame-duck pardon could sacrifice reputation, but that might be reclaimed over time. In sum, no president needs to apologize, much less answer for, their last-minute pardons. It is power without responsibility. Nonetheless, Trump did not pardon the January 6ers.

When Trump ran for president again, he cast the riot as an act of patriotism. "I call them the J-6 patriots," Trump told *Time*.[70] At rallies, his campaign played a video featuring the so-called "J6 Prison Choir"—a group of men incarcerated for their roles on January 6 whose habit was to sing "The Star-Spangled Banner" every night from their cells.[71] Reportedly, Trump played the track for a group of supporters at Mar-a-Lago in April 2023.[72]

Patriots deserve pardons, among a great many other tokens of gratitude. When asked whether he would consider pardoning every rioter, Trump said, "Yes, absolutely."[73] This was a weak promise. Later, he clarified, "I am inclined to pardon many of them. I can't say for every single one, because a couple of them, probably they got out of control."[74]

There were distinctions amongst the rioters. According to CNN, "some defendants are elderly people who got caught up in the frenzy and went in the Capitol but never attacked anyone or broke anything. Others viciously assaulted police with batons, chemical sprays, and baseball bats." Even pardon advocates thought such differences mattered. "Not everybody who went to the Capitol was a saint, right? So, you have to draw distinctions between people," argued Joseph McBride, a lawyer for January 6 defendants. "Even in the situations where people were violent, maybe a pardon is not the best idea, but maybe a commutation is." In any event, Trump simply had "to deliver" some clemency to his loyal supporters, said McBride.[75]

When you make promises on a campaign trail, sometimes wiggle room or nuance vanishes. Voters hear what they want to hear, and hopes grow. After the election, expectations for a broad pardon were at a fever pitch. "Unless the president pardons everybody, he is going to get some significant blowback," said John Pierce, a pro-Trump attorney who represented dozens of the January 6ers. "They are not a shy group of people."[76] History had proved as much.

Families also thought their loved ones were about to be liberated. "The only thing I could think of when I heard that Trump won the election was that my mom is coming home," said Savannah Huntington, daughter of Rachel Powell. Powell had been found guilty of multiple felonies and was entering the second year of a five-year jail sentence. But Huntington supposed, with reason, that Trump was going to grant a full pardon to her mother.[77] Who wouldn't pardon patriots?

Days before the inauguration, there were considerable doubts about the scope of the coming amnesty. The vice president-elect, J. D. Vance, discussed pardons for the January 6ers, distinguishing between those who were violent and those who were not. "If you protested peacefully on January 6 and had Merrick Garland's Department of Justice treat you like a gang member, you should be pardoned. If you committed violence on that day, obviously you shouldn't be pardoned."[78] Other Republicans drew the same line; violent offenders would not be pardoned.[79]

But once Trump entered office, he announced a momentous clemency: "This proclamation ends a grave national injustice that has been perpetrated upon the American people over the last four years and begins a process of national reconciliation." He began with a commutation of sentences for fourteen people. He went on to "grant a full, complete and unconditional pardon to all other individuals convicted of offenses related to events that occurred at or near the United States Capitol on January 6, 2021." Relatedly, he ordered the attorney general to dismiss pending cases "against individuals for their conduct related to the events at or near the United States Capitol on January 6, 2020."[80]

Democrats were uniformly critical of this amnesty. While some Republicans maintained a studied silence, a few GOP senators expressed mild disapproval. "Pardoning the people who went into the Capitol and beat up a police officer violently I think was a mistake, because it seems to suggest that's an OK thing to do," said

Lindsey Graham.[81] Tom Tillis said it was "surprising to me that it was a blanket pardon," and "I just can't agree."[82] Tillis perhaps meant that he was shocked that it covered the violent January 6ers. Susan Collins distinguished those who "got caught up in the crowd that day" and those who "assaulted police officers with their fists, with flag poles, with pepper spray, and destroycd property."[83] The latter group did not "warrant clemency."[84]

Trump's precise reasons for pardoning violent rioters are unclear. Some claimed that he had previously promised to pardon everybody. Trump implied as much after the decision: "I was very clear about it . . . I said I was going to release 'em. . . . And they voted for me and I won in a landslide. And that was only one of the many reasons."[85] But to my knowledge he never quite said he would pardon *everybody*, perhaps fearing that would make him seem to condone violence against police officers. He always left wiggle room to exclude the violent offenders.

Perhaps Trump really believed all the rioters were "hostages" or "political prisoners," and hence they were all similarly situated. After the decision, he said, "This was a political hoax. And you know what? Those people—and I'm not saying in every single case—but there was a lot of patriotism with those people."[86] He meant that they were targeted due to their devotion to him and their political principles.

Or perhaps Trump concluded his voters would be upset about pardons that distinguished the good January 6ers from the bad ones, with pardons only for the nonviolent. If you tell your supporters you are going to pardon the *nonviolent* January 6ers, they might overlook that qualification. During an interview after the pardon, Trump boasted of having provided the voiceover recitation of the Pledge of Allegiance on the J-6 Prison Choir track. "It was the number one selling song, number one on *Billboard,* number one on everything for so long. People get it. They wanted to see those people released," by which he perhaps meant that his base would not have appreciated a nuanced approach to clemency for the January 6ers.[87]

If we peek behind the curtain, news accounts recount internal debate prior to the pardon. Trump himself vacillated between targeted amnesty versus including some violent offenders. But as his advisers debated the issue, reportedly "Trump just said: 'F—k it: Release 'em all.'"[88] This sounds about right: a rash and unnuanced decision born of frustration.

Days after the pardon, Trump spoke to *Fox News:* "Most of the people were absolutely innocent. OK. But forgetting all about that, these people have served, horribly, a long time. It would be very, very cumbersome to go and look—you know how many people we're talking about? Fifteen hundred people."[89]

This was a hodgepodge. Were most "absolutely innocent"? Of course not. Trump's observation that "these people have served . . . a long time" sounded like a reason for a commutation, not a reason for a pardon. By focusing on the time they had already served in prison, he seemed to be conceding their guilt and complaining about the severity of the punishment.

I suppose that the actual reasons were a hodgepodge, as well. First, Trump likely sought to tar all the investigations and prosecutions as products of a thoroughly partisan process; drawing distinctions among the January 6ers might have undermined that goal by implying that not all the prosecutions were crooked. Second, he perhaps supposed that elements of his base wanted a pardon for all the rioters and that clemency for only the nonviolent January 6ers would have generated sustained pressure to pardon the rest. That would be unpleasant. If he was going to give in later, why not give in now? Finally, Trump did not want to wade through a thousand-plus cases. Nor did he want to wait for others to do so. That was too "cumbersome." Trump wanted to act swiftly, to say that he had fulfilled a promise on day one of his second term. You cannot have nuance, or individualized assessments, when you seek to act at warp speed. Only a sweeping amnesty could meet his desiderata. The breadth of the pardon was perhaps all but inevitable.

Unforeseen Complications and Unintended Breadth

The January 20 amnesty continues to reverberate in extraordinary, unprecedented, and unforeseen ways. For understandable reasons, some recipients read the expansive pardon expansively. Who wouldn't, given its loose expressions? They argued that the pardon covered more than entering the Capitol, violence against Capitol Hill Police, destruction of property within the Capitol, and the like. Specifically, recipients whose arrests led to the discovery of other crimes, such as illegal gun or drug possession, believed that those separate criminal actions were also pardoned.[90] The wording of the president's proclamation stated his desire to "grant a full, complete and unconditional pardon to all other individuals convicted of offenses related to events that occurred at or near the United States Capitol on January 6, 2021."[91] The question was: Were *other* criminal indictments stemming from investigation of January 6 offenses "related" to those events?

To Dan Wilson, they felt related. He had entered the Capitol on January 6, 2021. In 2023, the FBI came to his home and arrested him. During the raid, the government discovered illegal firearms in the house. In May 2024, Wilson pled guilty to one January 6 count and two firearm offenses. With Trump's January 20 pardon, Wilson was released from custody—but soon after, the government sought his rearrest to serve out the unrelated convictions. Wilson went to court to argue that the pardon applied to the firearm offenses, too. At this point, the government changed its position and agreed that Trump's January 20 pardon did cover offenses for which the defendant would not have been convicted but for his involvement in January 6.[92]

The district court denied Wilson's motion.[93] The DC Circuit agreed. The pardon "plainly applies to related offenses—not, as here, to an offense that is only connected to January 6 by the happenstance that it was uncovered during investigation of the unrelated January 6 offenses." The firearm offenses, said the court, "occurred at a different time and place, and the elements of these offenses—possession of an unlicensed firearm and the possession of firearms by a prohibited person—bear no relationship to conduct that occurred at the Capitol on January 6."[94] One judge dissented. She supposed that courts ought to defer to the executive's reading of its own pardon.[95]

The issue remains contested, with some judges adopting a broad reading of the January 20 amnesty.[96] This legal issue will continue to play out for months, perhaps even years, for many J6ers have ample reason to insist upon the broad reading. Complicating matters, the executive may have taken inconsistent stances on whether the pardon applies to unrelated offenses uncovered in the course of investigating and prosecuting January 6 actions. Based on news accounts, the executive has sometimes declared that such offenses are covered by the January 20 pardon, and at other times claimed they are omitted. Any inconsistency puts executive branch lawyers in a difficult position, as judges will likely highlight the discrepancy.

Interpreting pardons can be crucial, as they are not always crystal clear. Should the executive be able to decide the meaning of a pardon authoritatively? More modestly, should the executive receive deference to its reasonable reading of a pardon? Count me among the doubters. A pardon changes legal rights and duties. Once it issues, it vests certain rights upon the recipient, very much like a new law might. In my view, an executive pardon should be read as a congressional law would be. A year after a law is passed, we do not go back to the Congress that passed it to hear what it was thinking. Likewise, a month or a year after a pardon is granted, we should not blindly accept the president's reading. Of course, judges should give an executive's reading respectful consideration, just as they accord similar respect to all arguments in their courts. But attentive deliberation is quite different from blind acceptance.

If an executive asserts a narrow reading that is at odds with the best reading of the pardon, my view is that the executive should have been more careful in granting the pardon in the first place. We do not want second thoughts, or criticisms, to lead a president to argue for a limited reading of a pardon. Equally, if the executive espouses an expansive reading that seems at odds with the best interpretation, a court should not adopt that interpretation.

In any event, whenever the executive prefers an expansive clemency, there is a tool at hand: the president can take up her pardon pen and issue a new proclamation that reflects her current desires. Nothing prevents President Trump from granting another pardon for Wilson, and others, if that is what he desires. Rather than misreading the January 20 pardon, he should have issued a new one.

To be clear, I have no problem with interpreting pardons with due regard for the intentions of the presidents who issued them. I believe that the president's intentions at the time of the pardon should be taken into account. My concern is with post-hoc regrets about the breadth, or lack thereof, of a pardon. I do not suppose the president should be able to expand or contract a pardon like an accordion via interpretation months or years after the fact.

Pardons should be understood by reference to their original intent. A review of the January 20 pardon furthers that claim, because it contains numerous textual oddities. First, the pardon declares that the attorney general "shall ensure that all individuals convicted of offenses related to events that occurred at or near the United States Capitol on January 6, 2021, who are currently held in prison are released immediately."[97] But this directive cannot mean what it says. While the proclamation pardons certain offenses, it does not absolve the recipients of *all* crimes of which they have been convicted. If a January 6 pardon recipient were also serving time for a murder committed in some other place and time, it was not the president's intent—regardless of what the proclamation says—to release that prisoner merely because he had also been convicted for January 6 offenses. Given the president's evident intent, the Bureau of the Prisons should have released only those prisoners who were in jail solely due to offenses related to events that occurred at or near the US Capitol.

Second, despite the text of the pardon, the president did not mean to pardon individuals who committed a crime near the Capitol on January 6. If Thieving Tom robbed someone three blocks from the Capitol on January 6, 2021, and was convicted, there is a literal sense in which he is being punished for an offense "related to events that occurred at or near the United States Capitol on January 6, 2021." Nonetheless, it would be ridiculous to think that President Trump meant to pardon such a perpetrator, whose crime was wholly unrelated to the storming of the Capitol but happened to occur in the vicinity. Despite its text, the pardon was not meant to grant clemency to all who committed crimes "near the Capitol," but clemency only to those who committed crimes related to the riot on Capitol Hill. Further, the amnesty should not even be read to cover all crimes that occurred *at the Capitol* on January 6. If a thief stole a sightseer's phone inside the Capitol at nine o'clock in the morning on January 6, 2021, or a police officer punched a jogger on the Capitol's steps late that evening, one should conclude that the amnesty excluded both crimes. These are not offenses the president sought to pardon, having nothing to do with the storming of the Capitol.

If my readings are right, the president's January 20 pardon needs to be read more narrowly than the text of the pardon suggests. In my estimation, the president's amnesty says many things that the president could not have possibly meant, and hence a narrowing construction is necessary. The January 20 pardon should not be read literally.

"IT WAS A SAD day for Lady Justice no matter which side of the political spectrum you're on," said former US Attorney John Fishwick Jr., reflecting on the pardons of January 20, 2025. "In alternative ways, both Biden and Trump were sending the same message. Trump was saying it was a corrupt system the last four years, and Biden was saying it's about to be a corrupt system. And that's a horrible message."[98] In fact, Biden was also saying the system was debased, because he publicly said that federal prosecutors had targeted Hunter and that his son never should have been prosecuted. Senator Susan Collins spoke for millions when she said it had been "a terrible week for our justice system."[99]

One set of pardons would block future prosecutions; the other set overturned existing convictions. Each side pointed a finger at the other. Truth be told, both sides had a point.

CHAPTER 6

Our Pardon Dystopia

THE BIDEN AND TRUMP PARDONS suggest that we are in a new epoch, one where pardons are often, perhaps mostly, used as instruments of ordinary politics and widely seen as such. Of course, presidents will continue to recite traditional motives, like forgiveness and mercy. But the public, slowly inured to the politics underlying the most notorious pardons, will grow increasingly cynical. A new president will enter office and not only reverse executive orders but perhaps also nullify scores of his predecessor's prosecutions, especially the ones that can be painted as partisan and political. The lame-duck president, before leaving office, will seek to prevent prosecutions of the administration's allies, including White House aides and other officials who may soon be in the prosecutorial crosshairs. Indeed, presidents seeking to maximize their power might embolden their assistants with hints of pardons: "Do my bidding and I'll take care of you before I leave office."

Yet the January 19 and 20 pardons only scratch the surface of possibilities, for there are so many other ways in which clemency might advance politics and partisan aims. This chapter discusses some of the pardon controversies arising in the wake of Donald Trump's return to the White House. Others relate to Trump's attempts to cast doubt or nullify Joseph Biden's pardons. Still other potential storms loom ominously on the horizon, waiting for an entrepreneurial president to seize upon latent possibilities.

A Two-Tiered Pardon System

Because pardons are extremely valuable, the distribution of them matters. The public will prize a fair distribution of clemency over a biased one. Yet the current system seems inequitable because it favors the rich and the connected over the meek, the contrite, and the deserving. All other things being equal, those with connections to the president have noticeable and obvious advantages.

Consider the process. There are two paths to a pardon: the winding trail through the Department of Justice and the direct White House path. The former path is protracted, but open to all; the latter is short, but realistically available only to those with connections. The White House pathway has a low success rate. But the other route—the Justice Department's—has *even dimmer* prospects.[1] Those with connections and influence always choose the White House track and may never bother with the other.

The original system consisted of direct application to the president. Presidents received requests for clemency and made decisions about each. As the volume of applications increased over time, conducting presidential review became extremely challenging and time-consuming. In the nineteenth century, Congress designated assistants to aid the president. For a spell, the attorney general played that role, then a "pardon clerk" did, and then an "attorney in charge of pardons."[2] In 1894, Congress established the Office of the Pardon Attorney within the Department of Justice, an office that remains to this day.[3]

Today, most applicants file with the pardon attorney. The pardon attorney generally requires that pardon seekers wait five years *after* conviction or release date before applying.[4] The requirement depresses applications, as those who profess innocence must be incarcerated for an extended period before they can apply for clemency. Relatedly, the office accepts petitions for commutation only after the applicant has begun serving a sentence.[5]

When evaluating petitions, the pardon attorney considers five factors: "post-conviction conduct, character, and reputation"; the "seriousness and relative recentness of the offense"; "acceptance of responsibility, remorse, and atonement"; the "need for relief"; and "official recommendations and reports."[6] For commutations, the pardon attorney looks to the "disparity or undue severity of sentence, critical illness or old age, and meritorious service rendered to the government," such as cooperating with investigators.[7]

This process may take years. The sentencing judge and the US attorney's office that prosecuted the case are consulted, and their opinions are given "considerable weight."[8] Eventually, the pardon attorney makes recommendations to the deputy attorney general. Only the latter's positive recommendations are presented to the president.[9] In 2022, the Department of Justice (DOJ) had a backlog of over 18,000 cases.[10] And in 2024, the White House had a backlog of hundreds of people the DOJ had recommended for pardons.[11]

The DOJ's approval is neither sufficient nor necessary. First, the president can reject the department's advice to grant, no matter how sound that recommendation is. Second, even if the department opposes clemency, the president can grant it. Third, the president can pardon individuals who never submitted a petition to the pardon attorney.[12] In other words, presidents continue to do what they did in the earliest years of the Republic—receive and approve pardon petitions.

During the first Trump term, perhaps no more than 11 percent of the president's total grants (pardons, commutations, and so forth) arose from pardon attorney recommendations.[13] That means 89 percent of pardon applications lacked a positive recommendation from the DOJ.[14] The Biden Administration may have been much the same. In the final week of his administration, Biden granted clemency to nearly 2,500 individuals. According to an internal DOJ email, the DOJ had recommended only 258 of those grants, or about 10 percent.[15] Any applicant with a weak case for clemency might wish to bypass the pardon attorney, because that office's protracted and careful process would likely underscore the petition's flaws. An applicant who never applies to the DOJ may never receive its disapproval.

Dodging the pardon attorney means sending your application directly to the White House. Mailing an application to the White House will achieve nothing. Instead, you must convince senior White House officials to review your petition and then hope that they put it on the president's desk and schedule. Again, it seems that the most recent pardons were issued in this manner.[16]

Should presidents routinely sidestep the DOJ? One might suppose that the DOJ is hardly the ideal institution for vetting pardon applications. It is focused on prosecutions, and pardons nullify convictions. The DOJ's focus on prosecutions probably makes it somewhat reluctant to recommend clemency. A president who believed the DOJ was biased against clemency could ask Congress to relocate the Office of the Pardon Attorney outside of the DOJ. The current setup, with the DOJ expending considerable resources on petitions and the White House routinely ignoring or bypassing the DOJ, makes little sense.

The Pardon Lobby

If the president pardoned only on the recommendation of the Justice Department, as Jimmy Carter claimed to have done, the influence of outside lobbyists would be weak to nonexistent.[17] But Jimmy Carter was unusual in so many ways. While some of his successors may have admired the thoroughness of the Department of Justice, none have wished to serve as its rubber stamp. They have drawn their own conclusions and acted accordingly.

In some instances, presidents may dislike the DOJ's recommendations and involvement because, when pardon grants lack the DOJ's imprimatur, they may seem irregular or suspect. Elizabeth Oyer, who served as pardon attorney under Biden, was critical of his end-of-term pardons. Regarding some last-minute grants of clemency, Oyer wrote in an email that "the process by which yesterday's action [clemency] was carried out was not what we had hoped and advocated for." Further, she acknowledged that "some of the clemency grants are very upsetting."[18] No president would welcome these comments.

Oyer continued in her post during the first months of Trump 47 before being fired, allegedly for refusing to recommend clemency for actor Mel Gibson.[19] The firing might suggest that the White House disfavors a pardon attorney who exercises independent judgment but because Trump had decided to appoint a White House pardon "czar," Alice Johnson, we can assume that the sidelining of Oyer would have continued in any event.[20] Johnson herself had spent twenty years in jail for money laundering and drug crimes when, having been lobbied by Kim Kardashian, Trump pardoned her in his first term.[21] Her new role confirmed that the center of gravity for pardons would be the White House.

With increased White House staff influence over pardons seemingly coming at the expense of the DOJ, we can expect lobbyists to play a more powerful role. Lobbying for pardons goes back to England.[22] Knowing the right people made it easier to ensure that the Crown would consider and grant the pardon. Those who knew the right people could charge for their access. Eventually, Americans replicated the system. At least by the time of Abraham Lincoln and Andrew Johnson, there were "pardon brokers."[23] They advertised in newspapers, particularly in the South. Some of the most successful of them were female, called the "Lady Lobbyists at the White House."[24] Johnson's staff tried to discourage the business, writing that "any intimation that money can assist a petition is a gross insult."[25]

The lobbying endures, albeit on a grander scale. In 2025, some practitioners are quoting "well north of $1 million to put cases together and get them in front of the [Trump] White House." That was the rough estimate for lobbying on behalf of Sam Bankman-Fried, the fraudster behind the cryptocurrency exchange FTX. He has, of course, hired a lobbyist. Heading far north of that number, *The Wall Street Journal* reported that digital currency entrepreneur Roger Ver—known as Bitcoin Jesus—offered one lobbyist $5 million and two others $10 million. His associates urged him to pay as much as $30 million, but he balked at that amount. Ver hired Roger Stone, a friend of President Trump.[26] How much Ver will end up paying Stone is uncertain. Bitcoin Jesus has no pardon, yet.

No one can doubt that having connections to the White House is crucial for getting the president's attention. "You need someone who can get in front of the president for five minutes and make a pitch," said Eric Rosen, an attorney representing pardon applicants.[27]

Though any pardon seeker would benefit from an advocate, that does not quite mean that petitioners must hire and pay a professional lobbyist. Unpaid celebrities can also be effective influence peddlers. To get a pardon application in the hands of White House officials, one might recruit a celebrity who has attracted the president's attention—say, a Deion Sanders or Kim Kardashian.[28] A Hollywood actress or an Olympian might take an interest in a prisoner, galvanize fanatical admirers, and pressure the president for clemency. If a superstar takes up your cause, your petition will more likely receive White House consideration. It is the goal of modern presidents to win the news cycle, and they may dominate more cycles by periodically issuing pardons that gratify influencers. Presidents see the advantages of celebrities and their fans bestowing unstinting praise. Social media and the press will buzz with excitement about the president's mercy and humanity.

Because he was a celebrity before he became president, President Trump may have a particular affinity for celebrities and may be especially susceptible to their influence.[29] He surely knows that their gratitude and praise will generate glowing news coverage. Savvy pardon petitioners have figured all of this out. As one said, "I'll take *any* Kardashian" to champion the case.[30] There are many Kardashians available, and they all seem to crave publicity.

Along the same lines, a form of pardon that appears to have become more common during Trump's presidency is celebrity clemency.[31] Forgiving an actress, rapper, or boxer generates fawning coverage as that star's admirers applaud mercy for their cherished celeb, and the president basks in the adulation. If an idol's fans are delighted when their favorite secures a pardon for someone else, they will be over the moon when their icon is the recipient of a pardon.

Of course, pardons have always had a public-facing aspect. Recall that written pardons are addressed to the world, and they typically begin with a similar opening: "To all whom these presents shall come, Greeting." Pardoners, monarchs especially, have long granted clemency to burnish their public image.

The main point is that influence matters, whether paid for or not. One pardon official said this of the Trump process: "It seems that ordinary people who don't have the resources to hire a lobbyist . . . and [who] don't have political connections and access to the White House door are not being considered at all."[32] This does not seem an exaggeration.

Pardoning Corporations

If pardoning celebrities can generate some good press, it seems unlikely that pardoning corporations would have the same effect. Whatever their societal utility, corporations do not evoke much admiration or sympathy. Perhaps that partly explains why no president ever pardoned a corporation. That is, none *had* ever done so before March 2025. That month, Trump pardoned two: HDR Global Trading and Ozy Media.[33] HDR owed the US government $100 million in fines.[34] Ozy owed over $35 million in penalties.[35] Neither must now pay those sums.

Corporate pardons might seem especially problematic or suspect.[36] The amounts can be eye-popping. We must remember, however, that individuals may also owe substantial fines, penalties, and forfeitures, and these can be pardoned. Pardoning corporations does not present unique or worse consequences for federal revenue unless we assume that corporate sanctions are collectively higher than those imposed on individuals. Yet the ability to pardon corporations does make it more likely that the federal fisc will suffer significant losses, because the more sorts of fines, penalties, and forfeitures that the president can forgive, the worse the potential effects on the fisc.

The case for the presidential power to pardon corporations arises from the Pardon Clause. Corporations face fines, penalties, and forfeitures that can amount to billions of dollars. Because they can commit "offenses against the United States," the president can pardon these violations. History points in the same direction, as the Crown pardoned corporations as well.[37]

Cash for Clemency

Pardons are valuable. The dollar value of clemency will depend upon the wealth of the recipient and the sanction that is eliminated. To a billionaire who avoids prison time, a pardon or commutation might be worth more than $100 million. If so, the billionaire might spend tens of millions on lobbyists. There will be some ignominy from paying lobbyists and receiving a pardon, but if the billionaire receives clemency, it will seem money well spent.

From another standpoint—that of the private parties who seek restitution from the convicted—clemency can have serious drawbacks. In June 2025, Democratic staffers for members of the House Judiciary Committee estimated that by letting over sixteen hundred people off the hook, President Trump's pardons "could deprive the pardoned offenders' victims (and their survivors) of approximately $1.3 billion in restitution and fines owed to them and American taxpayers." One of Trump 47's pardon recipients, Trevor Milton, may have owed over $500 million.[38] Milton had been convicted of defrauding investors in his electric vehicle startup in 2022 and was awaiting a restitution order from a court. Prosecutors had recommended restitution of $680 million. If that was the proper amount and Milton had the funds to pay the restitution, Milton's pardon may have been worth something approaching half a billion dollars.

Knowing that there is money to be had, and that lobbyists are making lots of it, certain presidents might wish to cut out the middlemen and capture the gains themselves. Although English monarchs accepted payments for pardons, our system frowns upon a practice that seems akin to bribery. Some people have suggested that a recent Supreme Court case makes it possible for presidents literally to sell pardons.[39] I am not convinced that such assertions are correct. According to the court's opinion in that case, *Trump v. United States*, Congress could not make it a crime to pardon someone.[40] I do not think, however, that the Supreme Court implied it was lawful to enter a bribe contract. It explicitly noted that a president might be charged with bribery.[41] If the president agreed to a pardon in exchange for cash, that would violate the bribery statute, even if the president never granted a pardon.

But what is entirely common is donating to campaigns, super PACs, and presidential libraries. Furthermore, politicians routinely exercise their official powers—proposing a bill, voting on an amendment, appointing an officer, vetoing a bill, or crafting (or repealing) regulations—in ways that please, even delight, donors. Donations are not considered bribes unless the politician agrees to some official action in return. Without that agreement, there is no bribery.

The connection between donations and pardons has existed for at least twenty-five years. Recall that Bill Clinton pardoned Marc Rich—whose ex-wife, Denise Rich, had contributed $450,000 to Clinton's presidential library, $100,000 to his wife's Senate campaign, and over $1 million to the Democratic Party.[42] Also recall Jimmy Carter's reaction, saying it was clear that "some of the factors in his pardon were attributable to his large gifts." To him, the evident influence of these valuable contributions made Clinton's pardon "disgraceful."[43] These were harsh words coming from a fellow Southern Democrat.

President Clinton now has company. To return to Trevor Milton, he was convicted in 2022 of fraud in connection with the company Nikola. Later, Milton donated about $1.7 million to Trump's 2024 campaign. After Trump's inauguration, Milton stumped for a pardon, casting himself as a victim of prosecutorial abuse. In March 2025, Milton received a call. The caller ID displayed "Executive Office of the President of the United States." Milton thought it was "fake," but answered anyway. According to Milton, the president said, "It's signed. You're cleaner than a baby's bottom, you're cleaner than I am, Trevor."[44] When asked later, "Did you buy yourself a pardon?" Milton told his interviewer, "Oh heck no. I wouldn't even know how to do that, first of all. Second of all, it would be illegal to do."[45]

Were there links between these donations and pardons? It is hard to say for certain. Some observations and predictions, however, may be useful. First, as a general matter, donors appear to be buying access to politicians, in the sense that when donors contribute vast sums to campaigns they surely expect that, if issues arise on which they wish to be heard, they will get respectful hearings from those politicians. Access matters because it can place a donor's concerns on a politician's busy agenda. Politicians have limited bandwidth, and if you can capture the attention of a high-level politician, you increase the chances that she will view an issue in the way you do and act accordingly. One cannot obtain a presidential pardon unless pardon consideration is *on the president's schedule.* Hence, securing a spot on the president's calendar is of vast importance.

Second, although President Clinton's pardon of Marc Rich sparked an explosive scandal, that outrage might have dissipated as Americans became more cynical about our government. When Trump pardoned Mr. Milton, little outrage beyond the above-cited memo was expressed by Democrats or anyone else. There was a stir when, in 2021, a pardon-seeker told the *New York Times* that Rudolph Giuliani was willing to help people in his position for a fee of $2 million.[46] But in March of 2025, there was mostly silence following Trump's pardon of Milton. It may well be that Trump's second term was proving so newsworthy—between spending cuts, firings, tariffs, military actions, deportations, riots, and retaliations—that the Milton pardon got lost in the shuffle. Perhaps outrage is a limited resource and was directed at other scandals, real and imagined.

Third, cash for clemency is terrible. Yet I am unsure that it is any worse than donations for votes in Congress, donations for appointments to ambassadorial posts, and so forth. Legislators regularly propose legislation in line with contributors' interests, and more importantly, often vote in ways that gratify their donors.[47] Likewise, presidents appoint campaign bundlers to vital ambassadorial posts.[48] Both practices raise awkward questions, for one might conclude that the donations purchased the vote or the appointment. In response, politicians routinely say that, while they are grateful for the donations, et cetera, et cetera, their decisions have absolutely nothing to do with those vital contributions to healthy political debate. Politicians of all stripes reliably insist that their actions were guided by their understanding of constituents' priorities and the nation's best interests. They did not propose, vote, or appoint because some donors sought this or that.

The same can be said by presidents who issue pardons to financial supporters. All presidents may insist that their pardons are in the public interest, even if some pardon recipients happen to be campaign donors. Milton and Rich received their pardons because the president genuinely believed clemency was appropriate, or so presidents and their defenders will claim. To be clear, I am not trying to minimize the awfulness of cash-for-clemency. Instead, I am saying that all of these situations—clemency, legislation, and appointments—are equally troubling, because in every case observers are left to wonder whether a donation was a factor in a pardon, vote, or appointment.

Now, perhaps there are reasons to be *more troubled* by cash-for-clemency in particular. One might be that the president has a unilateral authority to pardon. And as we have seen, pardons can be extremely valuable. But presidents wield similar authority over appointments—and those are valuable, too. Imagine recess-appointing (temporarily installing) an extremely generous supporter and donor bundler to be the deputy secretary of state or the ambassador to the United Kingdom. Even the chance to hold the title for a short spell might send that donor over the moon. Furthermore, presidents may veto legislation in ways that further the interests of donors. Suppose that the president counts executives from the automobile industry among his campaign's most generous supporters, and uses the veto pen to squash legislation the industry vehemently opposes. All in all, I am not sure that pardons fundamentally differ from vetoes, appointments, or any other unilateral presidential decisions.

As for the donors, they are clever. Like Trevor Milton, they will deny that they bought a pardon. They will say that they merely exercised their constitutional right to donate to a campaign. The next pardon recipient might say, "I donated because I support the president's stance on Social Security, not to receive a pardon." If they are particularly cheeky, they might even say, "I donated millions to the presidential library because I examined the president's generous clemency policy and deeply admired what I saw. The president is full of mercy and genuinely believes in second chances." That is, after all, akin to what industries say of their donations to politicians: "We donated to Paula Politician because we greatly appreciate and value her stance on our industry."

It may be that we are on the precipice of a new era. Given the clemency granted to Milton, wealthy pardon-seekers will likely consider donating to campaigns and libraries. The observable fact of donors receiving the extra consideration that comes with contributions will reinforce the link between donations and clemency. Further, not many donors have to receive clemency for others to perceive that donations exert a positive influence on their chances. When the incumbent pays greater attention to a pardon-seeker who is also a donor, she need not feel awkward, much less dirty. The president can say to herself, "I already do that for donors who want to be ambassadors, who seek executive orders, and who desire regulatory changes. How is this any different?" If I am right, the appearance of cash for clemency is perhaps here to stay.

When Does a Pardon Vest?

We slide now from the tawdry to the perplexing. When we think of pardons, we imagine a document. Written instruments specify the pardon recipient, the breadth (commutation, remission, full pardon), and any conditions that the president wishes to attach. A written record can be produced for the jailer, the prosecutor, or the judge, thereby authenticating the claim of clemency.

But if written pardons are the norm and have obvious practical advantages, does that mean oral pardons are taboo?[49] There are stories from England of "verbal pardons," where monarchs forgave people without producing any documents.[50] I suppose the US Constitution permits such pardons. If a prisoner is about to be executed and the president calls the prison warden to stay the execution, that call amounts to a reprieve, even though it is oral. Likewise, if the president calls a penitentiary and personally tells the warden to "release your prisoner, Carlos de Contrite," that seems the equivalent of a written commutation. In either case, the warden might seek documentation, so that no one doubts the propriety of the action. But an understandable desire for a record hardly constitutes an argument that the Constitution requires a written instrument.

This issue seems academic, the stuff of law school hypotheticals. But the question came to life during Trump 45. In mid-December of 2020, the president spoke with representatives of a convict, James Rosemond, allegedly telling them that "he had decided to commute Mr. Rosemond's sentence" and telling his staff in the room, "Let's get this guy home for Christmas." Was this a commutation? Rosemond thought so and sought his release from prison. The district court rejected his argument, saying that pardons had to be in writing. The Fourth Circuit disagreed: Is "writing required as a part of the President's exercise of the clemency power[?] The answer is undoubtedly no." The Constitution imposed no such limit, and because it had no constraint the president might exercise the pardon power orally. Nonetheless, Rosemond lost because the court concluded that his evidence merely established a *desire* to commute at some point and was not itself a commutation or evidence of a prior commutation.[51]

As a constitutional matter, I think the Fourth Circuit was correct. But the difficulties of oral pardons are legion. There can be slips of the tongue, a chance that presidents sometimes say things without entirely thinking them through, and the real possibility of mistaken memories and concocted stories. The president might be under the misimpression of talking to one lobbyist while talking to another—and in that case, whose client is being pardoned? In a meeting, the president might be harangued into uttering something later regretted. Again, instruments can better specify the pardon recipient, the breadth of the clemency, and any conditions the president wishes to attach. Further, the recipient can produce a written pardon, and the executive can better maintain a record.

If oral pardons are constitutional, they are complete once the oral statement is complete. A president who utters: "I unconditionally pardon Alivelu Vaddiparti," has done what was said aloud. I do not think that the beneficiary needs to be within earshot. To be sure, the pardoned person cannot invoke the pardon if they are unaware of it. Yet, as noted earlier, the president can convey the decision to the prison warden and have the prisoner released, even without a written pardon.

When does a written pardon vest or become final? That issue arose in 2008. On December 23, President George W. Bush signed a master pardon warrant that pardoned, among others, Robert Toussie.[52] But the next day, the president decided not to have the pardon attorney issue an individualized pardon for Toussie.[53] The pardon had not gone through the regular process with the pardon attorney, said the White House. Further, the White House was previously unaware that Toussie's father had donated to the Republican Party. Bush clearly did not want a repeat of the Marc Rich fiasco, meaning he did not want people to suppose that he pardoned Toussie because of the donation. Based on their reading of Supreme Court cases, the White House took the position that, without physical delivery to Toussie, the pardon had never taken effect. This meant that Toussie had not been pardoned. But some scholars disagreed, arguing that Toussie had been pardoned and that physical delivery was unnecessary. I think the critics were right. A pardon reads as if the very act of signing grants the clemency: "I hereby grant a pardon . . ." So when the pardon is signed, the president has pardoned someone, even if the person never receives the pardon. Indeed, many pardons have been issued en masse, with no delivery because the clemency derives from the general grant. Think of America's repeated amnesties, where some members of the pardoned class never received individual pardons.[54]

To be clear, I think the president could condition a pardon's effectiveness on delivery and acceptance. The president could provide in his signed pardon that "I pardon Anthony Burlaza upon his acceptance of this offer." This would be a conditional pardon, one focused on acceptance. But most pardons say nothing about delivery to the person, much less their acceptance. Again, when the president signs a pardon that declares "I hereby grant a pardon," the president has done precisely what the pardon declares to the world.

Autopenned Pardons

In recent times, presidents have often used a machine called the autopen to affix their signatures to documents, including pardons. The autopen merely replicates the president's actual signature. The president decides what is to be done, and the staff affixes his signature with the autopen.[55]

The Executive Branch supposes that it is entirely legal for the president to skip an actual signature and use an autopen. [56] This seems like the correct view, as presidents have long used agents to sign on their behalf, and the autopen is simply a mechanical agent. Many people use automated signatures today, using companies like DocuSign. Why can't the president choose to sign something using a machine?

In 2025, President Trump called all this into doubt. He posted the following online: "The Pardons that Sleepy Joe Biden gave to [many] are hereby declared VOID, VACANT AND OF NO FURTHER FORCE OR EFFECT because of the fact that they were done by Autopen."[57] But President Trump has used the autopen for many documents.[58] He clearly does not believe that official acts need a manual signature. And there is no reason to suppose that pardons are subject to a unique rule of actual signature.

In any event, if oral pardons are valid, then a written pardon that is autopenned is generally good evidence of a completed pardon. The production of the pardon document *and* the president's decision to sign, via autopen or otherwise, seems sufficient to establish that the president has pardoned someone.

Given the volume of documents that the president signs (pardons, executive orders, proclamations, bills, and so forth) and the other vital work that the president must attend to, the autopen is not going anywhere. A president simultaneously navigating foreign crises, domestic political clashes, nomination struggles, routine law execution disputes, and any number of scandals, real or imagined, saves a fair amount of time by using a machine to affix a signature to legal documents.

Compos Mentis and Pardons

Official acts presuppose that officials are making decisions when of sound mind. We might question the validity of an act by a severely intoxicated president because of beliefs about the mental state necessary for making constitutional and statutory decisions. Likewise, a president in a coma is incapable of pardoning, even if a pen is placed in that executive's hand and manipulated to yield a signature.[59]

Given the mental deterioration of Joseph Biden during the last few years of his presidency, the Trump Administration is investigating the validity of the autopenned pardons issued in the last weeks of the Biden presidency.[60] Part of that inquiry will rest on whether Biden was, in fact, deciding whom to pardon, what to pardon, and on what conditions. Was President Biden making those choices or were other people making them without his genuine involvement?

This is a complex inquiry because it seeks to reconstruct what happened in the White House at specific moments on particular days, and it also forces us to confront challenging constitutional questions. Did Joseph Biden comprehend what was put in front of him for his approval? Did he know that Betty Bostock was to receive a full pardon, that Kerry Kim was to receive a commutation, and that Ahmad Anwar was to receive a remission of fines conditional on his acceptance of guilt? What if Biden knew that he was being asked to exercise his powers under the Pardon Clause, but he paid little attention to the intricate details of conditions and exceptions? What if he approved them without paying any heed to the fine details? Even if he was in full control of his mental faculties, it is quite possible that Biden did not fully understand all the details of what he was signing, given that many people trust others and sign documents without reading them. You and I do this all the time, signing contracts to buy candy bars, cars, or real estate. If we do this, one can imagine that presidents do it as well. They are signing things without reading them, including pardons. But does the Constitution forbid such decisions, and does it render the resulting pardons invalid? There are no easy answers.

Time will tell, but I doubt that the Trump Administration will find a smoking gun—evidence that pardons were issued without Biden's genuine approval. They are unlikely to find someone declaring that President Biden did not want to grant a pardon that was issued. And even if former President Biden were to say, "I did not want to pardon and I did not pardon" a person who received a written pardon from his administration, it is always possible that Biden's recollection is faulty. There is a reason that we have a Twenty-Fifth Amendment and a procedure for declaring the president unfit for office.[61] The failure to use it raises a host of questions about Biden-era decisions, but I suspect that most of the investigations will prove inconclusive.

There is one more wrinkle. This discussion assumes that Biden cannot hand off the pardon pen to others. But as we have seen, Governor Henry Lee of Virginia issued pardons for President Washington during the Whiskey Rebellion.[62] That episode suggests that the president may delegate the power to pardon. If pardon delegations are permissible and if Biden delegated the power to others, then Biden's mental state may not matter to the validity of the pardons. The difficulty, of course, is that while Lee openly issued pardons on the president's behalf, no pardon during the Biden administration was issued in anyone's name other than President Biden. Neither the White House chief of staff nor the attorney general purported to issue a pardon pursuant to a delegation. That suggests that Biden never delegated the pardon pen.

And yet President Biden and aides have claimed that the President "signed off on the standards he wanted to be used to determine which convicts would qualify for a reduction in sentence."[63] That is, the president adopted standards and his aides decided who fit those standards. That is a type of delegation, one that will be more or less significant depending upon the looseness or strictness of the standards. News accounts also say that after the application of the standards, the lists of clemency recipients was modified, apparently by aides and not by Biden himself.[64] This account, if true, suggests that aides did not quite apply his standards. If they pardoned fewer people, at least all pardon recipients met the standards set by the president. If they pardoned some people who did not meet Biden's standards, then something was quite amiss. One supposes that investigators will focus on the standards and how they were applied. And one further supposes that lawyers will have to consider the extent to which the Constitution allows presidents to delegate pardon discretion to subordinates.

Campaign Pardons

Trump's promise to pardon the J6ers, discussed in the previous chapter, was not the first time that a *candidate* for office promised clemency. Precisely when electoral promises to pardon first began is uncertain. Candidate Jimmy Carter telegraphed his future pardon of draft evaders in 1976. However, this was not a campaign ploy to garner votes, as the context makes clear. Before the American Legion, to a chorus of boos, Carter said he had struggled with his decision.[65] If this was a campaign maneuver, Carter would have addressed draft evaders (or a group more sympathetic to them) and not veterans, a group disapproving of "draft dodgers."

Perhaps Joe Biden was the first to promise a pardon explicitly. As mentioned earlier, in a bid to secure the youth vote, candidate Biden promised to "expunge" marijuana convictions, which sure sounds like a promise to pardon.[66] Sure enough, after President Biden issued his marijuana clemency in 2022, aides claimed that he had fulfilled "campaign commitments."[67] Newspaper accounts linked the 2022 pardon to, of all things, the president's student debt forgiveness.[68]

The reason? The youth of the nation were believed to both oppose marijuana criminalization and favor student debt relief. The 2022 midterm elections were just two months away at the time of the 2022 pardon. He was firing up his base with the marijuana pardon. He had to get them to the polls.

As with much else, Donald Trump takes the cake. As noted in the last chapter, in 2024, candidate Trump spoke of the January 6 defendants as "hostages." In March, he posted on social media: "My first acts as your next President will be to Close the Border, DRILL, BABY, DRILL, and Free the January 6 Hostages being wrongfully imprisoned!"[69] His supporters, and the American people, knew that he would free many, if not all, of the "hostages."

This raises the obvious question: Besides promises about jobs ("I promise to create ten million jobs") and promises about spending ("I vow to spend billions more on guns *and* butter"), will we now regularly see promises about clemency—commutations, remissions, and full pardons? Will a progressive candidate opposed to the "War on Drugs" pledge clemency for illegal possession of oxycodone, crack cocaine, and fentanyl? There are a lot of Americans—family and friends—with deep sympathy and understanding, and there are plenty of addicts. Making such a promise might move thousands (even millions) of voters. Or imagine a social conservative who promises to pardon soldiers involved in law-of-war offenses and police officers who committed federal crimes in the course of their official duties? There is a lot of admiration, even veneration, for people in uniform. The point is that candidates can harvest votes by promising to pardon sympathetic figures, whether they are in jail, on trial, or merely dreading arrest, trial, and punishment.

We may be on the cusp of a new era. Candidates may pledge to pardon people they perceive to be in their voting coalition. For Democrats, that might be young people or passionate environmentalists. For Republicans, it might be evangelicals or underemployed men. Given that we are in an era of shifting coalitions, one cannot say for certain. As compared to the many other promises that candidates make, these promises are *realistic*. Presidents cannot create jobs, maintain peace, or reduce the budget. Those all require help from God, good luck, or the intervention of Congress. But presidents can commute, remit, and pardon, which means they have the keys to a vast "goodie box" filled with unlimited forgiveness. Of course, I do not expect presidents to regularly pardon murderers or terrorists. Further, some will excoriate pardons that others loudly extol. But politicians can be expected to discern which pardons are electorally advantageous for them, and which are election-day poison. Presidents already promise the sun, the moon, the stars; increasingly, they will add free pardons to the long list.

Policy Pardons

As just observed, candidate Joseph Biden promised that he would "decriminalize cannabis use and automatically expunge prior convictions," as part of a broader criminal justice reform plan released by his campaign in July 2019.[70] In 2022 and 2023, President Biden redeemed that pledge, granting a sweeping amnesty for marijuana use and possession. The first pardon covered simple possession of marijuana, whether the persons were convicted or not.[71] In other words, it covered those found guilty and those who might yet be prosecuted. In his 2023 proclamation, Biden pardoned "additional individuals" who faced "collateral consequences" for possession, attempted possession, or use of marijuana. He also covered more federal and District of Columbia statutes.[72]

The president's reasons were not much related to mercy or a desire for calibration (making the punishment fit the crime). Rather, policy drove his decisions. In 2022, as he issued the amnesty, he declared his ringing opposition to the law's policy of putting people in jail for marijuana use and possession:

> As I often said during my campaign for President, no one should be in jail just for using or possessing marijuana. Sending people to prison for possessing marijuana has upended too many lives. . . . Criminal records . . . have also imposed needless barriers to employment, housing and educational opportunities. And . . . black and brown people have been arrested, prosecuted, and convicted at disproportionate rates.[73]

An official said the president was "taking steps" against the past "failed approach to marijuana." Legislators had been "working on this issue" but their efforts had "stalled," causing the president to act unilaterally. "This is a significant development," the official said, and one that "delivers on the President's campaign commitments."[74]

Ironically, in 2022, no one was in prison "solely for simple possession of marijuana."[75] I think this means that people were in jail for marijuana possession *and* other offenses. Because they were in prison for multiple offenses, no one was immediately released. Nonetheless, the amnesties were momentous—this truly *was* a "significant development." As President Biden liked to say, "I'm serious," and "No joke." As far as I know, this was the first pardon grounded on the president's *disagreement* with a federal law and the policy behind it. The president was saying, in effect, "I do not care for these laws" and "I don't believe there should be any consequences from violating them."[76]

The second policy-based clemency came in 2024, when Biden commuted almost all prisoners on death row, some 37 in total. The reason: "[The President] believes that America must stop the use of the death penalty at the federal level, except in cases of terrorism and hate-motivated mass murder—which is why today's actions apply to all but those cases."[77] This was a policy commutation too. Biden was (mostly) opposed to the death penalty and acted on that moral view in opposition to the laws of Congress.

As broad as postwar amnesties had already been, they were not issued in opposition to any laws. When President Jimmy Carter pardoned Vietnam-era draft evaders, he was not saying, "I think we should have no laws against draft evasion." During the campaign, he said it was time "for the damage, hatred and divisiveness of the Vietnam War to be over."[78] When two presidents pardoned Confederates, neither was saying, "I oppose the Union and believe it is wrong to punish traitors." Lincoln and Johnson opposed disunion and treason.

If I am right, Biden's marijuana and death penalty clemencies are qualitatively different than what preceded them. A president sworn to execute the laws used the pardon power expressly to *undermine* some statutes on grounds of policy. Again, this was not mercy, reconciliation, or even calibration. The clemencies were grounded on a policy rationale.

I do not deny that the president can have an enforcement policy when it comes to marijuana offenses. Perhaps that would mean deciding to forego bringing charges against those who merely possess marijuana or declining to seek the death penalty. Such decisions may also be grounded in policy rationales, such as the claim that the executive's limited resources (time, personnel, money) should be focused on more important matters. Murder, terrorism, assault—each seems more critical than marijuana possession, or so someone might reasonably argue. Likewise, capital cases are very resource-intensive, and some might suppose that funds would be better spent on other purposes—say, prosecuting more criminals. In that context, it might make sense to waive prosecutions of marijuana possession and forgo requests for death sentences in order to preserve limited resources for other prosecutorial or penological matters.

These pardons, however, granted clemency to individuals who were already convicted and sentenced. For Biden's marijuana pardons, the government had already expended considerable resources to secure marijuana convictions. The same is true for convicts on death row—much has already been expended. It is true that both acts of clemency saved expenses—incarceration expenses for marijuana users and litigation expenses for death row inmates. But should those expenses matter in the exercise of the pardon power? If they do, wouldn't every policy pardon be justified? Could a president say, "I do not think that the government should waste money jailing fraudsters, so I am freeing all of them"?

To concentrate the mind, set aside marijuana. Imagine a president who sincerely believes in a policy of open borders. Whether a libertarian or a progressive, this executive signs a pardon: "I hereby pardon all those who have crossed the border illegally." Or imagine a president who dislikes taxes—we've had a few. That president elects to pardon *all tax penalties* owed to the federal government, and declares a reason: "Taxes are too high as it is. We should collect all existing taxes, of course. But penalizing someone for not paying their taxes? Well, I am dead set against that. That is profoundly un-American."

In an era where presidents have vast legislative agendas, extending to the decriminalization of certain offenses (marijuana) and the mitigation of penalties (softening mandatory prison minimums), the pardon power could prove a powerful tool and be incredibly tempting. If the president thinks compulsory minimums for certain crimes are a problem—say, the crime of drug dealing—those can be eliminated with general commutations. If the president supposes that the business community should not face sanctions for legal violations related to labor or the environment, those penalties and forfeitures can be forgiven.

In sum, Biden's marijuana pardons and death penalty commutations open a brave (and frightening) new world of *policy pardons,* where the president is pardoning not because of a person's particular circumstances or because of a rare need to pacify rebels, but merely because the president disapproves of the underlying policy that the law reflects.

We can make the scenario more interesting and more troubling. Imagine that a president enters office and immediately pardons all (fill in the blank—border crossers, tax scofflaws, or polluters). The pardon is accompanied by the following: "All Americans should know that I will pardon everyone at the end of my term for these offenses. No one should go to jail, or pay a sanction, for these acts." Americans might believe there would be follow-through on the promise because, after all, the president utterly detests the law's underlying policy. Nothing in the Constitution expressly bars a pardon coupled with a promise to pardon. And then imagine the president making good on the promise. "Promises kept," the new administration might exult to cheering fans as the president signed the complementary pardon on the last day in office.

To me, this scenario approaches a *suspension*. A suspension of law is an announcement that the executive will not enforce or honor some lawful statutes. The Crown did this when it disliked certain Parliamentary laws. But this power was abolished by the English Bill of Rights.[79] The president was thought not to have this power, because it was never granted either in direct terms or via the grant of "executive power."[80] But a promise of a pardon announced at the beginning of the term and to be issued at the end has the practical effect of suspending the law during the president's term. People run the risk that the president will break that pledge. But if the existing offenders were pardoned upon inauguration, why would anyone doubt that more pardons would come for those who offended during the president's term? It is a virtual certainty that they will get a pardon in the end. To demonstrate resolve and credibility, the president can issue a policy pardon every six months or annually, providing more expeditious relief. All that is required is changing the dates and signing again.

Can the president do any of this? I believe that a policy pardon seems akin to a suspension of the law and is therefore unconstitutional. Further, a promise of an end-of-term pardon would be worse.

However, these issues are hardly clear-cut, and what the courts might say about this is far from certain. After all, the president is not *formally* suspending the law, as English kings used to do. In this case, the executive is instead issuing one (or more) pardons that collectively have the effect of suspending those laws that the president finds objectionable on policy grounds.

The First Family Comes First

Joe Biden's family pardons were unprecedented only in the sense that he pardoned multiple relatives. The first recipient of a family pardon was likely Mary Todd Lincoln's half-sister. Emilie Todd Helm was the widow of a Confederate general. Her 1863 visit to the White House sparked controversy. One aide quipped that a guest from "Secessia" (the Confederacy) had arrived.[81] She left with a pardon, issued under Lincoln's Proclamation of Amnesty and Reconstruction. As discussed in Chapter 4, the pardon was an open offer to Confederates who swore the oath that she did.[82] Was there any favoritism? No. Again, Lincoln offered a pardon to *thousands* of Confederates if they took the oath of loyalty; Helm took it and therefore qualified. But one suspects that Lincoln was delighted to grant this gift to his sister-in-law.

Roger Clinton Jr. was such a problem for the Clintons that the Secret Service code-named him "Headache." Right before leaving office in 2001, President Clinton granted his half-brother a full pardon for a 1985 drug-trafficking conviction. Roger Clinton had served his full prison sentence, so this pardon was less meaningful. But Roger's associations with pardons did not end there.[83] According to House investigators, he earned hundreds of thousands of dollars as a pardon lobbyist, including "at least $335,000 in unexplained traveler's checks" deposited into his account from abroad. Who was he lobbying? His brother. Roger had as many as thirteen clients, including a Gambino mob associate, all seeking his brother's mercy. Roger did hand a list to his brother, but President Clinton did not pardon those on it.[84]

Recall that Donald Trump granted clemency to his daughter's father-in-law: Charles Kushner is the father of Jared Kushner, Ivanka Trump's husband. In 2003, he was investigated for making illegal campaign contributions.[85] Charles's brother-in-law was a witness for the prosecution. Incensed, Kushner hired a prostitute to sleep with his brother-in-law, secretly filmed the encounter, and then mailed the tape to his sister. The brother-in-law and his wife turned the tape over to prosecutors. The US attorney called the case "one of the most loathsome, disgusting crimes" he had ever prosecuted. Kushner pleaded guilty to sixteen counts of tax evasion, one count of retaliating against a federal witness, and another count of lying to the Federal Election Commission.[86]

In December of 2020, all was forgiven. Kushner had completed his sentence, and the White House claimed that Kushner's extensive philanthropy made him deserving of a full pardon. But one suspects that being father-in-law to Ivanka undoubtedly mattered far more than any philanthropy.[87]

Last comes Joseph Biden. As noted in Chapter 5, Biden issued a blanket pardon for Hunter Biden, covering "all offenses," violent or not, over a decade.[88] On the eve of his departure from the White House, Biden pardoned siblings and in-laws.[89] These were slightly less broad, covering "all non-violent offenses" that may have occurred over a decade.[90]

Family pardons are invariably a toxic cocktail of favoritism and suspected guilt. First, there is an unshakeable sense that the president wielded his veto pen to favor his kith and kin. These decisions never reflect detached consideration. How could they? Second, as we have seen, observers often infer guilt from a pardon. Nonetheless, family pardons will never entirely disappear because presidents are not above using the office for personal gain. Sometimes their families will be unfairly accused, triggering appropriate presidential sympathies. Other times, sons, daughters, and sisters will have violated federal law.

President Biden's family pardons will make it easier for successors to take similar actions. Exclaiming that "he did it first," much in the way that a naughty child might on the playground, will help justify future family pardons. When considering presidential power, and what is constitutional, practices matter in the courts and in the court of public opinion.

Will Donald Trump pardon his children before he leaves office? It is hard to say. He likely does not love his children any less than Joe Biden loves his family. And he can equally say that they have been, and will be, dragged through vindictive investigations. Because he believes that Democrats have victimized him, he will have little trouble concluding that his opponents will train their sights on his sons and daughters, too, once he leaves the political stage. And given the oft-expressed view that parents can be forgiven for favoring their children, maybe Trump will suppose that the public will pardon him for any clemency for Ivanka or Donald J. Trump Jr. There will be a temporary storm, of course. But Donald Trump is always caught up in storms. And almost all of them dissipate with little to no long-term damage.

Self-Pardons

We have full pardons, conditional pardons, blanket pardons, and many other varietals. What about a "selfie"—a self-pardon? There is no practice of presidential self-pardons. Nonetheless, the issue has come up a few times in the past half-century, as Professor Brian Kalt has observed.[91] It arose during Richard Nixon's presidency (after the Watergate scandal) and during the George H. W. Bush presidency (after the Iran-Contra Affair). And in more recent times, it came up during the Trump and Biden presidencies. This recent pattern raises a question: Are modern presidents more prone to acts of crime? Are we more apt to unearth their offenses now than in the past? Or are Americans more fractured along party lines and more prone to seeing the worst across the partisan aisle? We despise (hate?) more and hence find more offenses. Maybe all the above are true.

As discussed in Chapter 4, Richard Nixon seemed to need a pardon in 1974. Nixon's close lawyers claimed he could pardon himself.[92] But the lawyers in the Justice Department told him he could not absolve himself "due to the fundamental rule that no one may be a judge in his own case."[93] Curiously, Justice Department lawyers did opine that the president might "declare that he was temporarily unable to perform the duties of his office." At that point, per the rules of presidential succession found in the 25th Amendment, the vice president would be acting president and could pardon the president. Then Nixon could resign or resume the presidency.[94] This was a fascinating marriage of fidelity to legal principles ("you can't do that") and brazen evasion of them ("but try this shameless and harebrained scheme").

As noted, the issue arose again at the end of the Bush Administration. Would George H. W. Bush pardon himself? Some thought he could, and others disagreed. The independent counsel investigating and prosecuting the Iran-Contra scandal (in which arms were traded for hostages) believed that self-pardons were impermissible. Whatever the case may be, it would have been "unprecedented chutzpah" for the president to pardon himself.[95]

It may yet happen, that moment of supreme chutzpah. Some thought that President Trump might have pardoned himself for January 6. Some thought Biden might engage in a bit of self-help. Pardoning his family members showed a great deal of nerve. Either could have thought, as many self-help books urge, "First, one must forgive oneself."

Does the Constitution permit this supreme act of self-help, a self-pardon? To set the stage, remember that presidents can commit crimes. If a president willfully underreported his income, he has committed federal tax fraud. If the sitting president, in his spare time, drag races in the streets of DC, he has committed the crime of reckless driving. (That's happened before, albeit with carriages. President Ulysses Grant was arrested and fined for reckless driving when he raced carriages on the streets of Washington, DC).[96] Now, the president enjoys certain absolute immunities, or so the Supreme Court held in 2024 in a case involving President Trump. Yet those immunities encompass only *certain* official acts. Furthermore, there is no immunity for *any* private acts.[97]

Returning to the question: One possible answer would be "yes—the president can pardon himself." The president can "reprieve and pardon offenses against the United States."[98] If he has committed such an offense, he may forgive himself. This argument is straightforward, grounded on the text. Further, if the president cannot pardon himself, he is the one person in the world who cannot be pardoned for federal offenses, so long as he serves as president. Why should he be uniquely burdened during his term, based on a theory of an implicit exception?

Yet there are counterarguments, ones that many find convincing. There is the generic claim that the president cannot use powers in self-interested ways, an assertion that says no government officers may use their powers for personal reasons. Further, there is a more specific legal maxim that no person should be a judge in his or her own case. A judge cannot be a party to a case *and* decide that same case. This is an ancient and powerful maxim of law.[99]

But judges decide cases all the time when they have an interest in the outcome, in the sense that they care quite a bit about which side wins. A pro-choice judge does not have to recuse herself in a case involving abortion. Relatedly, a judge who *wants* to decide the merits of a case first must grapple with whether she has the authority to hear the case. Yet her undoubted interest in the case does not disqualify her from deciding the question of her power to say what the law is. Judges always decide if they have jurisdiction.[100]

Furthermore, branches often decide other matters of self-interest. A judge decides whether a party is contemptuous and worthy of a judicial sanction.[101] Imagine if you could punish people who were rude to you. Judges can do that, which is quite a power. Similarly, even though members of Congress work for us, they decide their own pay.[102] Surely they are self-interested. Relatedly, federal legislators often decide to exempt themselves from certain federal statutes.[103] We could go on and on.

The point is that each branch has powers that can be wielded in self-interested ways. And we do not ordinarily conclude that there is an implied exception when it comes to self-interested exercises. We do not say that Congress can set salaries for the courts and the executive branch, but not for itself. Congress decides its salaries. And we do not say that someone else should decide whether the courts have the authority to decide a particular case. Judges decide these questions, often concluding that they have the power to adjudicate the case. So, perhaps the president can decide to pardon himself on the theory that it is no odder than legislators setting their salaries and judges deciding the bounds of their judicial authority.

Is there a federal precedent for a self-pardon? Not by the president, yet. But there is one from the territories of the United States, where Congress created a territory and granted the territorial governor power to "grant pardons and remit fines and forfeitures for offenses against the laws of said Territory, and respites for offenses against the laws of the United States until the decision of the president can be made known thereon."[104]

A territorial governor used that power, similar to the president's authority, to grant clemency to himself. Washington Territory Governor Isaac I. Stevens was fighting an Indian war and had arrested men he believed to be aiding the Indians.[105] He held these men without trial. Lawyers sought their release, invoking the privilege of the writ of habeas corpus (the lawyers wanted the court to inquire into the detention's legality.) Under the Constitution, the executive has no authority to detain people indefinitely; it must charge or release prisoners.[106] The lawyers succeeded when the court issued a writ demanding the production of the prisoners.

Stevens went to the extreme, choosing to declare "martial law." Courts were shuttered and judges were arrested at the governor's behest. A judge eventually found the governor in contempt and fined him fifty dollars.[107] On July 10, 1856, Stevens issued this act of clemency:

> To all persons to whom these presents shall come Greeting, Know ye!. . . .
> That I[,] Isaac I. Stevens Governor of the [Washington] Territory by virtue of the authority vested in me as Governor as aforesaid in order that the President of the United States may be fully advised in the premises and his pleasure known thereon, do hereby, respite the said Isaac I. Stevens defendant from execution of said judgment and all proceedings for the enforcement and collection of said fine and costs until the decision of the President of the United States can be made known thereon.
> In testimony whereof I[,] Isaac I. Stevens as Governor of the Territory of Washington on this Tenth day of July AD 1856 . . . have set my sign manual and have caused the seal of said Territory to be affixed.
> Isaac I. Stevens, Gov. Ter. Wash.[108]

This was a respite, not a pardon. But the power to issue either was grounded on a congressional statute not much different from the Pardon Clause.

The judge reviewed the pardon and ordered the arrest of the governor. At that point, "friends [of the governor] paid the fine."[109] What principle was established? Hard to say. The judge may have thought that the act of clemency had no legal effect. In contrast,

Stevens perhaps supposed that language akin to the Pardon Clause permitted self-reprieves.

I confess that the more I think about self-pardons, the less comfortable I am with the conclusion that presidents can self-pardon. But my discomfort with this use of power does not mean that the Constitution forbids it. And one can imagine situations where many might think it entirely justified. Consider the following: a departing president feels that he is not guilty of violating any law. Yet he is certain he will be prosecuted, a trial which will be bad for him and terrible for the country. The prosecution will inflame passions, yield furious cries of partisanship, and lower America in the eyes of the world. To avoid this parade of horrors, he pardons himself and does so with the utmost sincerity. Depending upon your political priors, Joseph Biden could have sensibly thought this in 2025. And Donald Trump could have sensibly thought this in 2021. Both sides believe the other is weaponizing prosecutions; the sad truth is that both sides seem right.

Pardons and Faithful Execution

The president must "take care that the laws be faithfully executed"[110] and swears to "faithfully execute" the presidency.[111] These twin duties might be thought to constrain the pardon power. He cannot grant pardons that violate either his duties regarding law execution or his office.

The first duty–law execution–seems quite constraining, but it is not. To be sure, the president must execute the laws, not disregard or ignore them. But the effect of the faithful execution duty on the pardon power seems rather weak. When presidents pardon the innocent or pardon to stave off future law violations, such as by granting amnesty for rebels, the president is perhaps acting to further faithful law execution. But the problem is that presidents long have issued other sorts of pardons, ones that seem antithetical to the faithful execution of the laws. More often than not, when the president concludes that mercy is appropriate, he is essentially declaring that the laws are too inflexible or are too severe. Whether the president is saying there are extenuating personal circumstances, that the punishment does not fit the crime, or that the prisoner has suffered enough, the president is *obviously not executing the underlying laws of Congress.* If a criminal is sentenced for ten years pursuant to a federal law and the president commutes the sentence, the president is not honoring the law under which the criminal received a ten-year sentence. If the president pardons someone guilty, the same point holds, for the law requires the guilty to be punished according to the law. Pardons or commutations in any of these situations seem to be inconsistent with a duty of faithful execution, for these pardons necessarily undo or preclude the punishment that Congress requires by law.

All in all, most pardons or commutations do not cohere with the duty to take care that the laws be faithfully executed. One could say that so much the worse for our presidents and their faithfulness. Or one might say that reading faithful law execution into the pardon power would unduly circumscribe and cripple that power by imposing constraints that greatly decrease the utility of the Pardon Clause. It is one thing to say that the president should be circumspect when pardoning; it is a bridge too far to say that calibration or mercy for the guilty are unconstitutional due to the perceived implications of the duty of faithful law execution.

The second duty—faithful execution of the office—is likewise not much of a constraint. If the president issues a pardon having concluded it is in the interests of the United States, one might conclude that the president has faithfully executed the office. Presidents usually will be able to say, truthfully, that their actions were taken in pursuance of the interests of the United States. And, in any event, they rarely, if ever, admit that their acts are *not* in the national interest. Others may insist that certain acts, including pardons, are not in the national interest, but such claims will not have any practical effect. Courts are unlikely to second-guess whether pardons arc consistent with the presidential oath, much less whether they are in the interests of the United States.[112]

There is a broader problem with reading the faithful execution duties as if they constrained the pardon power. Perhaps the Pardon Clause constitutes something of an express right to act contrary to principles of faithful execution. In other words, maybe the pardon power serves as an implicit constraint on, or exception to, faithful execution of laws and the presidency. I do not endorse this view. But it is no more plausible than the assertion that two clauses constrain the pardon power. Indeed, there is a rule of interpretation that the specific will control the more general and there seems little doubt that the Pardon Clause is more specific than the Faithful Execution Clause or the Presidential Oath. If we must choose between these claims, the notion that the Pardon Clause takes precedence better fits our practices and longstanding pardon traditions.

The Problem of Unconstitutional Pardons

People can reach different conclusions about self-pardons or the Faithful Execution Clause's constraints on the Pardon Clause, yet the question remains of what to make of supposed pardons that are constitutionally invalid. If the president pardons someone before they commit a crime or pardons a *state* crime, neither pardon would be valid. Presidents cannot immunize in advance of an offense, and they cannot pardon state offenses. If one concludes that self-pardons are likewise unconstitutional, the answer is the same—there may be a document that has all the usual indicia of validity, issued by the president for the president—but it has no legal effect because it is a nullity. Executives and courts can ignore it.

Nonetheless, unconstitutional pardons may have real-world effects. If a president ever issued a self-pardon, many might deny its validity. But prosecutors would have to wonder whether any prosecution would prove fruitless. Even if they believe that the pardon is not worth the paper it is written on, the courts might disagree.

If the courts disagree, the prosecutor has expended resources and has potentially embarrassed herself. Knowing this, some prosecutors may elect to forgo charges when confronted by a pardon that they believe is an unconstitutional nullity. If an unconstitutional pardon has that effect, it has granted the recipient a measure of protection despite its unconstitutionality. In other words, notwithstanding their invalidity, unconstitutional pardons may have real-world effects that are exceedingly useful to the intended beneficiary.

Furthermore, if a president were to pardon herself and was not subsequently prosecuted, there might be some confusion as to the reasons. Did the prosecutor's independent judgment lead to the conclusion that no prosecution was warranted? Or did the pardon play some small or significant role in the decision? If the president is not prosecuted, and many suppose she ought to be, then some will conclude that the pardon made all the difference. But, of course, if no one wishes to prosecute the former president, then the pardon really had nothing to do with it.

My general points are that pardons can have real-world effects even if their validity is questionable. And they can be seen as having such effects even though no official paid them any heed. Sometimes practical effects and perceived influences matter more than the legality (or not) of some governmental action.

WE ARE AMID FUNDAMENTAL changes, perhaps a paradigm shift. There has always been a tendency to grant pardons to the connected, friends, and allies. Lady Justice might be blind, but presidents are not. You don't have to have friends in high places, but it sure helps.

Yet something has qualitatively changed over the past two presidencies. First, the process has become less concerned with mercy, reconciliation, or calibration, and far more focused on crass political calculations. As noted, the center of gravity has moved from the Department of Justice to the White House. While the DOJ may have a bias against granting pardons, because they undo the department's principal work, it focuses on contrition, mitigating circumstances, and other traditional pardon factors. The White House, however, has different priorities. The White House is more likely to think of pardons through the lens of optics, partisanship, and politics. Without the filtering mechanism of the DOJ, favors, contributions, and political calculations are far more likely to move the president. The president will want to favor friends and allies—he knows their intrinsic goodness and knows how much they have suffered (or will suffer). Further, the president will favor potential pardons that secure favorable press.

Second, the pardon pen will prove tempting to presidents stymied by Congress and the courts. As in other areas, presidents will push the boundaries of the Pardon Clause outward, seeking to advance personal, policy, and party interests. One cannot assume unmitigated success. But if the past is prologue—if presidents have expanded their war powers, foreign affairs authorities, and legislative authority—there is little reason to suppose that presidents will have less success when it comes to the Pardon Clause. We have seen presidents fulfill campaign promises to pardon, thereby reinforcing the idea that the pardon pen should be an instrument of politics—both electoral politics and promises kept. We might see presidents essentially suspend statutes by pardoning the guilty. Biden's marijuana and death penalty pardons point the way. Maybe next time, it will be tax laws, immigration statutes, or environmental laws. We cannot say for certain.

Third, the pardon pen will be used to undo and to protect. An incoming president will undo whatever prosecutions the previous administration undertook that its base perceives as partisan or unfair. Trump's January 20 pardons set the example. But, in a way, so did Biden's January 19 pardons. The latter pardons were grounded on the assumption that Trump would weaponize prosecutions and those who made that assumption are no doubt going to continue to view certain prosecutions during Trump 47 through that lens. When the next Democrat wins the White House, expect pardons for the victims of any perceived Trump inquisition.

Of course, Biden's pardons on January 19, 2025, also point the way for Trump. When he was last president, there was speculation that Trump would immunize the J6ers and allies. But Trump refrained from doing so, an uncharacteristic act of self-restraint. In 2029, as he departs office, Trump will not hesitate to shield friends and family. They will press him, and in his last moments of wielding the pardon pen, he will surely gratify some. Maybe he will even pardon himself and bring to a head that lingering question about self-pardons.

Welcome to our pardon dystopia, where the prerogative of mercy is an instrument of common politics and pardons are the continuation of politics by other means. Pardons will shield and reward allies, advance policy goals, and become crucial election ploys.

CHAPTER 7

The Future of Twenty Words

Our political house seems hopelessly divided, and in this period of discord, it is worth recalling another fraught time. In 1858, Abraham Lincoln addressed the Illinois State Republican Convention in Springfield, giving what has come to be known as his "House Divided" speech. He began his speech with sage advice: "If we could first know where we are, and whither we are tending, we could then better judge what to do, and how to do it."[1]

Today, many believe that constraints are necessary because they suppose that presidents have abused the pardon pen to reward allies and friends, to advance deeply contested policies, and to serve their narrow interests. For decades, a disturbing pattern has emerged as presidents depart from office. The lame-duck pardons the well-heeled, cronies, and ideological allies—miscreants who seem undeserving. A loud uproar erupts, full of dismay and hand-wringing, often from both sides of the political aisle. With the January 19 and January 20 pardons, a new dysfunctional norm may take hold. The outgoing president will pardon cronies and allies, as before. Going forward, the incoming president will take the presidential oath and may immediately fulfill campaign promises to pardon. If this latter prediction comes to pass, many observers will grow more firm in the belief that we must check the president's pardon power. *Indeed, some might suppose that we should abolish the pardon power entirely.*

But other experts have a different sense of what ails us, and we have not paid attention to this group of critics. Some criminal justice reformers suppose that we need more clemency. As one of them put it, "More people deserve a second chance."[2] To these critics, the president should intervene more often to prevent or halt miscarriages of justice—the wrongful convictions and the excessive and cruel punishments. If you suppose three-strikes laws are draconian—because minor offenses trigger major prison terms—you will favor more commutations. If you think the death penalty is imposed in a biased manner, you will want presidents to commute death sentences. To these critics, presidents are not dispensing enough mercy or doing much in the way of proper calibration.

I am unsure about this latter set of concerns. Sometimes I firmly believe that the federal government over-criminalizes and punishes too harshly. Other times I am amazed that criminals are treated with kid gloves. When it comes to pardons, my view is that we need fewer misguided or unjust pardons and more praiseworthy ones. I recognize that people will differ as to which pardons are deplorable and which are commendable and long overdue.

Below, I first consider the provocative assertion that we should abolish the pardon pen. Then I turn to idea that we ought to impose checks on the presidential pardon pen. Finally, some reformers may imagine that we need fewer *presidential* pardons and more pardons issued by others. I discuss how that might be possible. You are free to choose which reforms to support. Of course, we must recognize that there are downsides to any overhaul. Even if we could agree about what ails us, there is no silver bullet that will solve all of our pardon problems.

No Presidential Pardon Pen

Some ardent reformers might favor the outright abolition of the presidential pardon pen. To them, the existing pardon regime may seem too regal, too absolute, and too alarming. Why should one person be able to fling open the prison doors, (temporarily) end the death penalty, and shower favors on friends and family? Such abolitionists also might point out that a unilateral pardon power seems inconsistent with the general structure of checks and balances that permeates the Constitution. Finally, pardon abolitionists might suppose that others can take up the pardon pen, say Congress. If We the People abolish the presidential pardon pen, we can also ensure that others may exercise it, subject to appropriate constraints.

I regard this reform as akin to throwing out the baby with the bathwater. I suppose it makes sense to retain a presidential pardon power, albeit checked in one or more ways. While some presidential pardons seem misuses of the pardon pen, and this book has focused on those, I do not believe that most acts of presidential clemency are abusive. Further, I agree with William Blackstone that the pardon power appropriately rests with the institution empowered to execute the laws. In Britain that was the Crown. Under the US Constitution, the entity who executes the laws is the president and so he likewise should play a significant role in pardon issuance. I would not be so quick to obliterate the presidential pardon power.

Checking the President's Pen

If we seek to constrain the presidential pardon pen, then we must focus on which checks are necessary and how to institute those checks. Restraints can be internal or external.

Internal checks might consist of pardoning only those people recommended by the pardon attorney or the attorney general. Self-constraint might entail submitting all potential pardon grants to the presidential cabinet, and only proceeding with those that garner majority support. Self-constraint might consist of an ironclad refusal to pardon friends and family. Those people will be out of luck (for a period), but the rest of us will have greater confidence that access to clemency is not a matter of friendship or blood.

Unfortunately, self-restraint is as likely as July snow in Las Vegas. Self-constraint seems exceedingly unlikely because most presidents have little interest in limiting their own power and discretion. Presidents are unlikely to promulgate and abide by reforms that constrain presidential clemency, even if they agreed, in the abstract, that some restraints are necessary. They are apt to suppose that while other presidents should be checked, the checks should not apply to them.

External statutory restraints might be more efficacious, in theory. But we might wonder whether statutory checks are constitutional. The Supreme Court has said that Congress cannot limit the pardon power. The principle extends back to *United States v. Klein*, a post–Civil War case.[3] But in 2024, the Supreme Court summed up its understanding of the president's pardon power:

> [I]n 1870, . . . Chief Justice Chase held [a] provision [of law] unconstitutional because it "impair[ed] the effect of a pardon, and thus infring[ed] the constitutional power of the Executive." [The Klein Court continued,] "To the executive alone is intrusted the power of pardon," and the "legislature cannot change the effect of such a pardon any more than the executive can change a law." The President's authority to pardon, in other words, is "conclusive and preclusive," "disabling the Congress from acting upon the subject."[4]

It would seem to follow that Congress cannot limit the effect of a pardon, or decree that some federal offenses are no longer pardonable, or constrain when a pardon may be issued, or bar the president from forgiving friends and family. Hence it would seem that Congress cannot provide by law that the president may commute sentences but not pardon. Likewise, it would seem that Congress cannot declare that a lame-duck president shall not grant clemency after an election. The Supreme Court's reading of the Constitution makes the president more powerful than the British Crown of the eighteenth century, for while Congress cannot regulate the presidential pardon power by statute, the British Parliament certainly could do so.

In the short term, a Supreme Court reversal, one where it sanctions a congressional authority to regulate pardons, seems rather unlikely. Again, the quote above, which is highly protective of the presidential pardon, is from 2024. But the more the abuses pile up, the more tempting it will be for the court to reconsider its precedents and pronouncements. Stay tuned.

No one doubts that a formal constitutional amendment could constrain the presidential pardon pen. I am simplifying a bit here, but formal amendments require a two-thirds vote in both chambers and three-fourths approval by the states.[5] Given that modern presidents dominate their parties, we can expect them to lean on co-partisans in Congress and press them to reject attempts to curb a pardon power. The president's congressional allies are unlikely to insist upon an amendment that the incumbent resists. Given that both chambers usually contain sizable contingents of co-partisans, and given the high threshold for passage (two-thirds of each chamber), any meaningful presidential opposition will likely doom any amendment to limit the pardon power.

There is a strategy that would diminish, perhaps even eliminate, presidential opposition. The amendment can contain an effective date that begins after the incumbent leaves the White House. More precisely, Congress could delay the effective date of any pardon amendment for four or eight years. In that context, the incumbent might choose to remain silent about it. That would make passage of the amendment more likely. The point is that constitutional reform of the pardon power can be structured to mute or soften any opposition from the incumbent.

What constitutional reforms might be on the table? The possibilities are endless. One could require approval by the Senate, by the Cabinet, or by a new Clemency Committee. Think of it as "advice and consent" for pardons. The first proposal might prove burdensome on the Senate, for it seems sclerotic as is. The second would be a feeble check, because the modern Cabinet seems submissive, bordering on sycophantic. Would they ever say no to their boss, the president? Unlikely. The Clemency Committee would face opposition because it would create a new constitutional institution, and the appointment and tenure of its members would prove crucial to its ability to serve as an effective check. Over two centuries, Americans have shown little appetite for the creation of new constitutional institutions.

An alternative reform would establish something of a legislative veto on clemency. The president would have the power to grant provisional clemency. If either the Senate or the House disapproved within thirty (or sixty) days of the grant (excluding days Congress is not in session), the clemency would be ineffective. If both chambers said nothing within the relevant period, the pardon or commutation would take effect. When a president's clemency was truly awful, we could expect legislators to be galvanized, and one chamber might well disapprove. They might be especially willing to disapprove the last-minute pardons of a lame-duck president.

These first two reforms would leave the president with the initiative but subject the pardon power to a check before it was finalized. A third amendment possibility would deny the president the power to pardon certain offenses, such as murder or treason. Alternatively, an amendment might grant Congress the authority to decide which offenses the President could not pardon. The theory behind either of these reforms is that no single person should be able to pardon certain offenses. For especially troubling crimes, perhaps Congress ought to wield the pardon pen precisely because we desire fewer pardons of such offenses.

A fourth constitutional reform would bar pardons of family members, executive officials, and self-pardons. This option also carves out exceptions to the pardon power, ones which reflect concerns of favoritism and self-interest. This reform recognizes that presidents are predisposed to favor certain figures, and eliminates that bias by eradicating the power to pardon those persons.

Finally, one might suppose that there are periods during the presidential term where dispensing clemency seems inappropriate.

Perhaps lame-duck presidents should be barred from granting clemency after a presidential election. If the post-election period is generally thought to be particularly susceptible to abuse, then eliminating clemency during that phase might be a worthy reform. Or perhaps presidents should be prohibited from granting clemency six months before an election, lest pardons be exploited to secure contributions and votes.

These reforms can be combined and tailored in various ways. We might wish to impose a Senate check on pardons and also bar pardons by late-term, lame-duck presidents. We might bar family pardons and impose a legislative veto on death penalty commutations. And so on.

These reform proposals barely scratch the surface. An exhaustive review of state and foreign constitutions would suggest further avenues worth exploring. This is not the place to explore how other governments check the pardon power. But there is no doubt that we would learn a great deal from such an investigation.

More Pens, More Pardoners

If you want more pardons, one solution is straightforward. Create more pardoners. That is, create additional pardon institutions, each with a relatively free hand to grant mercy.

If you can swing a constitutional amendment, perhaps grant pardon authority to the justices of the Supreme Court, or the House speaker, or to a panel of eminent persons whose sole job it is to weigh pardon applications. You will get more clemency because, while the president would retain the power to pardon, others might grant clemency, as well, and therefore pardon people that the president declined to pardon. Think of it as the equivalent of the teen who is told "no" by one parent and then asks the other, often getting a different (more positive!) answer.

As discussed, passing an amendment is extraordinarily difficult. Yet, there are more mundane ways to increase the number of pardons. Perhaps the president, or Congress, can establish more pardoners.

First, maybe the president can unilaterally delegate the power to pardon. Recall that during the Whiskey Rebellion, Virginia Governor Henry Lee issued a federal amnesty, citing "powers and authorities" granted by President Washington.[6] Graham Dodds notes two other instances where lower-level executives granted clemency in furtherance of presidential objectives. He also notes that Lincoln was told that he could not delegate the power.[7]

Is the pardon power delegable? British practice suggests so. George III authorized his agents in America to grant pardons to rebels who would reattach themselves to Great Britain.[8] George's colonial governors had the power to pardon, as well.[9] It appears that British monarchs frequently delegated their power to pardon.

But that was under the more flexible British Constitution. Does the US Constitution authorize a president to delegate his pardon power? It is hard to say. The Constitution does not expressly authorize presidents to delegate the pardon authority or any other power for that matter. Nor does the Constitution affirmatively prohibit it.

I suppose three answers are possible. First, the Constitution implicitly authorizes presidents to unilaterally delegate the pardon pen. This would suggest that if President Washington delegated pardon authority to Governor Henry Lee, the first president did nothing constitutionally amiss. Second, one might suppose that chief executives cannot delegate the pardon power because the Constitution implicitly bars any delegation of the pardon pen. Some have argued that the pardon power is non-delegable and if they are right, then Governor Lee had no legal authority to grant federal clemency to anyone. Third, one might believe that the president can assign the pardon pen only when Congress statutorily authorizes presidential delegation. This theory imagines that while presidents lack constitutional authority to delegate the pardon pen, Congress can grant such power to them.

I do not have a firm view on the challenging question of presidential delegation. However, I will note that modern practices contain traces of delegation. Presidents sometimes issue multiple pardons via either proclamations or master warrants of pardon.[10] The proclamation or master warrant grants clemency to many named people or pardons a class (say, draft evaders). The president then instructs someone else (the pardon attorney) to issue individualized certificates of pardons. Trump did this for the J6ers, and Biden did this for marijuana users.[11] This instruction can effectively delegate some clemency authority. For Trump's J6 pardons, the pardon attorney could have read the language in the proclamation—"offenses related to events that occurred at or near the United States Capitol on January 6, 2021"—in many ways.[12] The greater the judgment and discretion that the pardon attorney wields in crafting the individualized pardons, the greater the implicit delegation. If the pardon attorney reads the president's instructions expansively, the DOJ might issue more pardons, each of which forgives more crimes. If the pardon attorney reads the president's directions more narrowly, the DOJ will issue fewer individualized pardons, each of which forgives fewer offenses.

Second, whether or not the president can delegate, perhaps Congress can grant pardon authority to others. Tellingly, Congress has long done so. Starting with a law from 1790, and many subsequent laws, Congress gave the treasury secretary the power to remit various tax forfeitures and penalties.[13] In 1885, the Supreme Court upheld the pardon grant, saying a continuous practice established its validity.[14] Relatedly, Congress has long granted various military commanders the power to pardon offenses committed by soldiers and sailors.[15] Finally, in 1910, Congress granted parole boards, acting under the authority of the attorney general, the power to parole offenders.[16] This was a form of conditional commutation, using a word, *parole,* long associated with a requirement of future good behavior. Well-behaved prisoners were told they could leave prison and remain free if they did not commit other offenses. For our purposes, the point is that parole boards, acting with the attorney general, could commute sentences without the knowledge or approval of the president.

These statutory grants raise an interesting question: Can Congress grant clemency authority over the president's objections? More precisely, could Congress, by veto-proof majorities, grant the Secretary of Defense or the Chief Justice the authority to reprieve and pardon? Or are the statutory grants constitutional only so long as the president continues to favor the grant of clemency authority to her subordinates? I do not know of a situation where Congress granted pardon authority over a presidential veto. But I have not reviewed every time a statute of Congress authorized others to grant clemency.

For the moment, assume that the president can delegate, that Congress can grant statutory authority to the president to delegate, or that Congress can vest pardon authority via statute. If any of these three regimes are constitutionally permissible, we open up interesting possibilities for other officers to wield a pardon pen. That power might come from a delegation from the president or an act of Congress. Imagine a pardon attorney who did more than review applications and make recommendations. Imagine a pardon attorney issuing pardons *without prior presidential approval.* This might be the best reform, because having a person dedicated to a task might make them better at it. Specialization has its advantages. More frequent and thoughtful use of the pardon power might result because, unlike the president, the pardon attorney would be *focused* on exercising it. So long as the president retained a concurrent power to pardon, there perhaps would be no constitutional difficulty.

Of course, any delegation or grant of the pardon pen would mean that some persons will receive clemency even though they would have never received any mercy from the president. On the one hand, the president might sometimes be rather displeased by the pardons issued by others. Given the examples above, where the treasury secretary and military commanders could grant clemency, this has always been a possibility. On the other hand, a pardon agent might grant pardons that the president would have approved in a world where the president had more time to consider all the pardon applications. In other words, sometimes, a pardon agent will helpfully advance the preferences of the president.

If concentration of power is a concern, create a pardon commission, composed of five or more members, where a majority may issue clemency. And if you want more pardons, create *two* pardon commissions, each of which may forgive. Again, the more people or institutions that can grant pardons, the more mercy, calibration, and reconciliation we will see. Of course, we also will see more annoyance and exasperation. What some see as calibration, mercy, or reconciliation, others might regard as miscalibration, coddling, and injustice.

* * *

If we are in a pardon dystopia, there will be no easy fixes. If we make it more difficult for the president to pardon, we might mitigate one problem—the politicization of pardons—at the expense of mercy, calibration, and reconciliation. If we create other pardoners, we might generate too many pardons and run the risk that these new institutions become just as politicized as the White House. We must never forget that our presidents *reflect and are a symptom of* the heightened partisanship and politicization that diffuses society.

But perils are no excuse for inaction. Perhaps things will have to get even worse before they can be made better. Winston Churchill is said to have observed, "you can always count on Americans to do the right thing—after they've tried everything else." Whether true or not, there is a compliment within the complaint. The tribute is that America will do the right thing. It might just take a bit of time as we stumble and blunder. Eventually, we are sure to exit our dystopia. We will not enter a pardon utopia, by any means. But normalcy, with its sporadic storms, is not so bad.

NOTES

ACKNOWLEDGMENTS

INDEX

Notes

Preface

1. US Const., art. II, § 2, cl. 1.

2. William Blackstone, *Commentaries on the Laws of England: A Facsimile of the First Edition of 1765–1769*, vol. 4, *Of Public Wrongs* (Chicago: University of Chicago Press, 1979), 390.

3. William Shakespeare, *The Merchant of Venice*, Act 4, Scene 1.

4. James Madison, Federalist no. 51, *The Federalist, with Letters of Brutus*, ed. Terrence Ball (Cambridge: Cambridge University Press, 2003), 251–252.

5. "Biden Issues Federal Pardons for 'Simple Possession' of Marijuana," *BBC News*, October 7, 2022, https://www.bbc.com/news/world-us-canada-63166964; Deepa Shivaram, "Biden Expands Pardons for Marijuana Possession and Grants Clemency to 11," *NPR*, December 22, 2023, https://www.npr.org/2023/12/22/1221230390/biden -pardons-clemency-marijuana-drug-offenses.

6. "Most Americans Favor Legalizing Marijuana for Medical, Recreational Use," Pew Research Center, March 26, 2024, https://www.pewresearch.org/politics/2024 /03/26/most-americans-favor-legalizing-marijuana-for-medical-recreational-use/.

7. Ben Schreckinger, "Biden Insists He's Not Involved in His Family's Business Dealings. But His Aides Are a Different Story," *Politico*, June 8, 2024, https://www .politico.com/news/2024/06/08/joe-biden-aides-family-business-dealings -00161476; Matt Viser, "Hunter Biden's Career of Benefiting from His Father's Name," *Washington Post*, November 18, 2024, https://www.washingtonpost.com /politics/2023/11/18/hunter-biden-family-name/.

8. Joseph R. Biden Jr., "Executive Grant of Clemency, Robert Hunter Biden," December 1, 2024, https://www.justice.gov/d9/2024-12/biden_warrant.pdf.

9. Joseph R. Biden Jr., "Executive Grant of Clemency, James B. Biden, Sara Jones Biden, Valerie Biden Owens, John T. Owens, Francis W. Biden," January 19, 2025, https://www.justice.gov/pardon/media/1385756/dl?inline.

10. "Biden Issues Pardons to His Family Members in Final Act in Office, Citing 'Unrelenting Attacks' from Trump and Allies," *PBS News*, January 20,

2025, https://www.pbs.org/newshour/politics/biden-issues-pardons-to-his-family-members-in-final-act-in-office-citing-unrelenting-attacks-from-trump-and-allies.

11. Juliegrace Brufke and Mary Ann Akers, "Trump Slams 'Crying' Liz Cheney and Frees J6 'Hostages,'" *Daily Beast,* January 20, 2025, https://www.thedailybeast.com/trump-slams-crying-liz-cheney-and-frees-j6-hostages/.

12. Matt Gluck and Jack Goldsmith, "Trump and the Pardon Attorney," *Lawfare,* July 6, 2021, https://www.lawfaremedia.org/article/trump-and-pardon-attorney.

13. "Trump Pardons Alice Johnson, Whose Cause Was Backed by Kim Kardashian," Reuters, August 28, 2020, https://www.reuters.com/article/world/trump-pardons-alice-johnson-whose-cause-was-backed-by-kim-kardashian-idUSKBN25O2R2/; "Lil Wayne and Kodak Black: Why Did Donald Trump Grant the Rappers Clemency?," *BBC,* January 20, 2021, https://www.bbc.com/news/entertainment-arts-55730190.

14. Viola Flowers, "Here Are All of the Celebrities Trump Has Pardoned So Far," *NBC News,* May 29, 2025, https://www.nbcnews.com/news/us-news/are-celebrities-trump-pardoned-far-rcna209736.

15. The Editors, "Pardoning Capitol Rioters Is No Way to Restore Law and Order," *National Review,* January 21, 2025, https://www.nationalreview.com/2025/01/pardoning-capitol-rioters-is-no-way-to-restore-law-and-order/.

16. Matt Dixon, Ryan J. Reilly, Peter Nicholas, and Katherine Doyle, "Trump Pardons Drive a Big, Burgeoning Business for Lobbyists," *NBC News,* May 31, 2025, https://www.nbcnews.com/politics/donald-trump/trump-pardons-drive-big-burgeoning-business-lobbyists-rcna209801.

17. Katherine Faulders, Rachel Scott, and Hannah Demissie, "Trump's Flurry of Pardons Include Some to Campaign Contributors," *ABC News,* May 29, 2025, https://abcnews.go.com/US/trumps-flurry-pardons-include-campaign-contributors/story?id=122313284.

18. Carl von Clausewitz, *On War,* trans. Col. J. J. Graham, vol. 1 (London: Kegan Paul, Trench, Trubner, 1918), 37.

19. US Const., art. II, § 2, cl. 2.

20. US Const., art. II, § 2, cl. 2.

21. US Const., art. II, § 3.

22. For discussion of increasing presidential proclivities to bend or ignore statutory law, see Saikrishna Bangalore Prakash, *The Living Presidency: An Originalist Argument Against Its Ever-Expanding Powers* (Cambridge, MA: Belknap Press of Harvard University Press, 2020), 215–245.

Chapter 1 · An Eighteenth-Century Clause

1. Matthew 27:15–26 (King James); Mark 15:6–15 (King James); Luke 23:18–25 (King James); John 18:39–40 (King James).

2. See, for example, Richard Wellington Husband, "The Pardoning of Prisoners by Pilate," *American Journal of Theology* 21, no. 1 (1917): 110–116.

3. Patrick D. Gaffney, *The Prophet's Pulpit: Islamic Preaching in Contemporary Egypt* (Oakland, CA: University of California Press, 1994), 176–177; Ayman S. Ibrahim, *Muhammad's Military Expeditions* (New York: Oxford University Press, 2024), 194–195.

4. Erin Bernstein and Kisari Mohan Ganguli, *The Mahabharata: A Modern Retelling*, vol. 3, *The Forest* (Munich: BookRix GmbH, 2017), ch. 346.

5. Ludo Rocher, *Studies in Hindu Law and Dharmaśāstra* (London: Anthem Press, 2012), 354.

6. See Restoration of Rights Project, "50-State Comparison: Pardon Policy and Practice," updated July 2024, https://ccresourcecenter.org/state-restoration -profiles/50-state-comparisoncharacteristics-of-pardon-authorities-2/.

7. Peter King and Richard Ward, "Rethinking the Bloody Code in Eighteenth-Century Britain: Capital Punishment at the Centre and on the Periphery," *Past and Present* 228, no. 1 (2015): 159–205, 184; Simon Devereaux, "The Bloodiest Code: Counting Executions and Pardons at the Old Bailey, 1730–1837," *SOLON Law, Crime and History* 6, no. 1 (2016): https://pearl.plymouth.ac.uk/solon/vol6/iss1/2.

8. Royal Household, "The Coronation Regalia," British Monarchy website (royal .uk), April 9, 2023, https://www.royal.uk/coronation-regalia.

9. William Blackstone, *Commentaries on the Laws of England: A Facsimile of the First Edition of 1765–1769*, vol. 4, *Of Public Wrongs* (Chicago: University of Chicago Press, 1979), 390.

10. George Washington, General Order, September 22, 1775, in *The Papers of George Washington, The Revolutionary War Series*, vol. 2, ed. W. W. Abbot (Charlottesville: University Press of Virginia, 1983), 35 and n.1 (hereafter *Washington Papers, Revolutionary War Series*).

11. Blackstone, *Commentaries*, 390.

12. George Washington, General Order, November 21, 1775, in *Washington Papers: Revolutionary War Series*, vol. 2, 413, 414.

13. Joseph Story, *Commentaries on the Constitution of the United States* (Boston: Hillard, Gray, 1833), 344–345.

14. George Washington to Brigadier General Francis Nash, August 17, 1777, in *Washington Papers, Revolutionary War Series*, vol. 10, ed. Philander D. Chase (2000), 652; see also George Washington to Brigadier General Anthony Wayne, November 27, 1779, *Washington Papers, Revolutionary War Series*, vol. 23, ed. William M. Ferraro (2012), 468 ("We do not see the multiplying of executions produce the effects for which they were intended; and for many reasons it is not a desirable thing to lose men in examples of this kind, unless in cases of the most apparent necessity").

15. George Washington, General Order, February 24, 1780, in *Washington Papers, Revolutionary War Series*, vol. 24, ed. Benjamin L. Huggins (2012), 562.

16. Alexander Hamilton, *Federalist* no. 74, *The Federalist, with Letters of "Brutus,"* ed. Terence Ball (Cambridge: Cambridge University Press, 2003), 363.

17. W. H. Humbert, *The Pardoning Power of the President* (Washington, DC: American Council on Public Affairs, 1941), 9.

18. Blackstone, *Commentaries*, vol. 4, 391–394.

19. See K. J. Kesselring, *Mercy and Authority in the Tudor State* (Cambridge: Cambridge University Press, 2003), 83–89, 131–133.

20. Kesselring, *Mercy and Authority in the Tudor State*, 61–62.

21. Kesselring, *Mercy and Authority in the Tudor State*, 62, 133.

22. See, for example, David Johnston and Don van Natta Jr., "The Clinton Pardons: The Lobbying; Clinton's Brother Pursued Clemency Bids for Friends," *New York Times*, February 23, 2001.

23. Kesselring, *Mercy and Authority in the Tudor State*, 14–15, 41, 58, 60–61, 64.

24. Kesselring, *Mercy and Authority in the Tudor State*, 58.

25. William F. Duker, "The President's Power to Pardon: A Constitutional History," *William and Mary Law Review* 18, no. 3 (1977): 475–538, 518; Kesselring, *Mercy and Authority in the Tudor State*, 61.

26. Christen Jensen, *The Pardoning Power in the American States* (Chicago: University of Chicago Press, 1922), 1–8; see also Evarts Boutell Greene, *The Provincial Governor in the English Colonies of North America* (Cambridge, MA: Harvard University Press, 1898), 124–126.

27. Blackstone, *Commentaries*, 4:390.

28. NY Const. art. XVIII (1777); Del. Const. art. VII (1776); Md. Const. art. XXXIII (1776); NC Const. art. XIX (1776).

29. NH Const. pt. II, cl. 40 (1784); Mass. Const. pt. II, ch. 2, § 1 art. VIII (1780); NJ Const. art. IX (1776); Va. Const. cl. 29 (1776); Vt. Const. ch. 2, § 11 (1786) (including the chief executive on the executive council); Pa. Const. § 20 (1776).

30. SC Const. art. XXX (1776); SC Const. art. XI (1778).

31. Edward McCrady, *The History of South Carolina in the Revolution 1775–1780* (London: Macmillan, 1901), 215.

32. Ga. Const. art. XIX (1777), emphasis added.

33. Ga. Const. art. XIX.

34. Ga. Const. art. II, § 7 (1789).

35. See, for example, Mass. Const. pt. II, ch. 2, § 1, art. VIII (1780); NC Const. art. XIX (1776).

36. Del. Const. art. VII (1776); NC Const. art. XIX (1776); Va. Const. cl. 29 (1776).

37. Mass. Const. pt. II, ch. 2, § 1, art. VIII (1780); NH Const. pt. II, cl. 40 (1784); NJ Const. art. IX (1776); NY Const. art. XVIII (1777).

38. NY Const. art. XVIII (1777); Vt. Const. ch. 2, § 11 (1786); Vt. Const. ch. 2, § 18 (1777); Pa. Const. § 20 (1776).

39. Mass. Const. pt. II, ch. 2, § 1 (1780); NH Const. pt. II, cl. 39 (1784); Pa. Const. § 20 (1776); Vt. Const. ch. 2, § 18 (1777); Vt. Const. ch. 2, § 11 (1786); SC Const. art. II, § 7 (1790).

40. See Bradley Chapin, *The American Law of Treason: Revolutionary and Early National Origins* (Seattle: University of Washington Press, 1964), 62 (describing Virginia legislature's general pardon); Charles D. Rodenbough, *Governor Alexander Martin: Biography of a North Carolina Revolutionary War Statesman* (Jefferson, NC: McFarland, 2004), 124 (North Carolina legislature granting a general pardon to separatists); "An Act for Pardoning Certain Offences Committed in the North-Eastern Parts of this [New York] State, Passed the 14th April, 1782," in *Journals of the Continental Congress, 1774–1789*, vol. 22, ed. Gaillard Hunt (Washington: Government Printing Office, 1914), 282–283 (hereafter *Journals of the Continental Congress*); "An Act for Pardoning the Persons Therein Described, on the Conditions Therein Mentioned," in *Journals of the Continental Congress*, vol. 31, ed. John C. Fitzpatrick (1934), 836–837 (South Carolina Act).

41. See, for example, Va. Const. cl. 29 (1776).

42. See, for example, NC Const. art. XIX (1776).

43. See David P. Szatmary, *Shays' Rebellion: The Making of an Agrarian Insurrection* (Amherst: University of Massachusetts Press, 1980), 84.

44. *Journals of the Continental Congress, 1774–1789*, vol. 10, ed. Worthington Chauncey Ford (1908), 381–382; *Journals of the Continental Congress*, vol. 22, 334–335.

45. David Lee Russell, *The American Revolution in the Southern Colonies* (Jefferson, NC: McFarland, 2000), 309.

46. Rodenbough, *Governor Alexander Martin*, 124.

47. Margaret Burnham Macmillan, *The War Governors in the American Revolution* (New York: Columbia University Press, 1943), 177–178.

48. Patrick Henry to Mayor of Richmond, January 13, 1785, in *Patrick Henry: Life, Correspondence, and Speeches*, vol. 3, ed. William Wirt Henry (New York: Charles Scribner's, 1891), 267, 268.

49. Macmillan, *The War Governors in the American Revolution*, 178n53.

50. Articles of Confederation of 1781, art. V.

51. Articles of Confederation of 1781, art. VI, art. IX.

52. *Journals of the Continental Congress*, vol. 8, ed. Worthington Chauncey Ford (Washington, DC: Government Printing Office, 1907), 550; *Journals of the Continental Congress*, vol. 9, ed. Worthington Chauncey Ford (1907), 1067.

53. *Journals of the Continental Congress*, vol. 2, ed. Worthington Chauncey Ford 1905), 122; *Journals of the Continental Congress, 1774–1789*, vol. 3, ed. Worthington Chauncey Ford (1907), 383.

54. Bruce Chadwick, *George Washington's War: The Forging of a Revolutionary Leader and the American Presidency* (Naperville, IL: Sourcebooks, 2005), 160–162.

55. Chadwick, *George Washington's War*, 461.

56. George Washington, General Order, February 6, 1783, *The Writings of George Washington from the Original Manuscript Sources, 1745–1799*, vol. 26, ed. John C. Fitzpatrick (Washington, DC: US Government Printing Office, 1938), 102–103; George Washington, General Order, July 4, 1779, *Washington Papers, Revolutionary War Series*, vol. 21, ed. William M. Ferraro (2012), 342 (granting release to all soldiers awaiting execution).

57. "The Virginia Resolutions, 29 May," in *The Documentary History of the Ratification of the Constitution*, vol. 1: *Constitutional Documents and Records, 1776–1787*, ed. Merrill Jensen (Madison: State Historical Society of Wisconsin, 1976), 243–245.

58. *The Records of the Federal Convention of 1787*, ed. Max Farrand, 3 vols. (New Haven: Yale University Press, 1911), 1:292 (hereafter Farrand's Records). Although Charles Pinckney later claimed to have proposed a pardon power that seemed remarkably like the one found in the Constitution, his actual proposal may not have included any enumerated pardon power. Compare Farrand's Records, 3:595–601, 3:604–609. Nonetheless, his generic grant of "executive authority" would have encompassed a pardon power. Farrand's Records, 3:599.

59. See Farrand's Records, 3:611–613.

60. Farrand's Records, 2:419.

61. Farrand's Records, 2:411, 419; compare the Act of Settlement passed by the Fifth Parliament of William III in 1700 (12 & 13 Will. 3, c. 2) which states "That no pardon under the great seal of England be pleadable to an impeachment by the commons in parliament." See also Ex Parte Wells, 59 US 307, (1855), 312–313 ("The provision in our constitution, excepting cases of impeachment out of the power of the President to pardon, was evidently taken from that statute [Act of Settlement], and is an improvement upon the same").

62. Farrand's Records, 2:426, 626–627.

63. Farrand's Records, 2:626–627.

64. Saikrishna Bangalore Prakash, *Imperial from the Beginning: The Constitution of the Original Executive* (New Haven: Yale University Press, 2015), ch. 1 (discussing why so many regarding the presidency as an elective monarchy).

65. Samuel Bryan, "Centinel I, Independent Gazetteer, October 5, 1787," in *The Documentary History of the Ratification of the Constitution*, vol. 2, *Pennsylvania*,

ed. Merrill Jensen (Madison: State Historical Society of Wisconsin, 1976): 158–167, 164–165. "Cato IV, *New York Journal,* November 8, 1787," in *The Documentary History of the Ratification of the Constitution,* vol. 19, *New York,* ed. John P. Kaminski and Gaspare J. Saladino (Madison: State Historical Society of Wisconsin, 2003), 195, 196.

66. "Convention Debates, July 30, 1788," in *The Documentary History of the Ratification of the Constitution,* vol. 30, *North Carolina,* ed. John P. Kaminski, Charles H. Schoenleber, et al. (Madison: State Historical Society of Wisconsin, 2019), 403–430, 414.

67. Luther Martin: Genuine Information IX, Baltimore Maryland Gazette, January 29, 1788, in *The Documentary History of the Ratification of the Constitution,* vol. 11, *Maryland,* ed. John P. Kaminski, Charles H. Schoenleber, et al. (Madison: Wisconsin Historical Society Press, 2015), 212, 214.

68. "George Mason's Objections to the Constitution of Government formed by the Convention, Oct. 7, 1787," in *The Documentary History of the Ratification of the Constitution,* vol. 8: *Virginia,* ed. John P. Kaminski and Gaspare J. Saladino (Madison: State Historical Society of Wisconsin, 1988), 43, 44; see also "Cato IV, New York Journal, November 8, 1787," in *The Documentary History of the Ratification of the Constitution,* vol. 19, *New York,* 195, 196.

69. "Centinel I, Philadelphia Independent Gazetteer, October 5, 1787," in *The Documentary History of the Ratification of the Constitution,* vol. 13, ed. John P. Kaminski (Madison: State Historical Society of Wisconsin, 1981), 326, 335.

70. "Convention Debates, July 30, 1788," in *The Documentary History of the Ratification of the Constitution, Volume 30: North Carolina,* 403–430, 414.

71. James Iredell, "Marcus III, *Norfolk and Portsmouth Journal,* 5 March," in *The Documentary History of the Ratification of the Constitution,* vol. 16, ed. John P. Kaminski and Gaspare J. Saladino (Madison: State Historical Society of Wisconsin, 1986): 322–326, 322–332.

72. "A Native of Virginia: Observations upon the Proposed Plan of Federal Government, April 2, 1788," in *The Documentary History of the Ratification of the Constitution,* vol. 9, *Virginia,* 655–697, 681.

73. Hamilton, *Federalist* no. 74, 362.

74. Hamilton, *Federalist* no. 74, 362.

75. Hamilton, *Federalist* no. 74, 363.

76. Hamilton, *Federalist* no. 74, 363–364.

77. "Convention Debate and Proceedings, July 19, 1788," in *The Documentary History of the Ratification of the Constitution,* vol. 23, *New York,* ed. John P. Kaminski and Gaspare J. Saladino (Madison: Wisconsin Historical Society Press, 2009),

2233, 2240 ("the Executive shall not grant pardons for treason, unless with the consent of the Congress").

78. "The Dissent of the Minority of the Pennsylvania Convention, Pennsylvania Packet, December 18, 1787," in *The Documentary History of the Ratification of the Constitution,* vol. 15, ed. John P. Kaminski and Gaspare J. Saladino (Madison: State Historical Society of Wisconsin, 1984): 7–35, 30.

Chapter 2 · Parsing the Pardon Power

1. Abraham Lincoln, *The Collected Works of Abraham Lincoln,* vol. 8, ed. Roy P. Basler (New Brunswick, NJ: Rutgers University Press, 1953), 412.

2. Lincoln, *Collected Works,* 8:103.

3. US Const., art. II, § 2, cl. 1.

4. Ex Parte Wells, 59 US 307, 314 (1855).

5. Ex Parte Wells, 314.

6. Ex Parte Wells, 315.

7. *United States v. Wilson,* 32 US 150, 160 (1833).

8. Ex Parte Garland, 71 US 333, 380, 381 (1866).

9. *Nixon v. United States,* 506 US 224, 232 (1993) ("the granting of a pardon is in no sense an overturning of a judgment of conviction by some other tribunal"— meaning that the fact of conviction remains undisturbed).

10. *Osborn v. United States,* 91 US 474, 478 (1875) (discussing power to remit penalties and forfeitures).

11. Proclamation No. 37, 13 Stat. 758 (May 29, 1865).

12. Noah A. Messing, "A New Power?: Civil Offenses and Presidential Clemency," *Buffalo Law Review* 64, no. 4 (2016): 661–743.

13. US Const., amend. V; amend. VI; amend. VIII.

14. US Const., amend. V.

15. Messing, "A New Power?" 729–730.

16. Messing, "A New Power?" 678.

17. *Pollock v. Bridgeport Steam-Boat Co. (The Laura),* 114 US 411, 413–414 (1885), emphasis added.

18. *Sessions v. Dimaya,* 584 US 148, 184 (2018), Gorsuch, J., concurring.

19. Messing, "A New Power?"

20. Messing, "A New Power?," 729–730, 742.

21. Messing, "A New Power?," 719–721.

22. William Blackstone, *Commentaries on the Laws of England: A Facsimile of the First Edition of 1765–1769,* vol. 4, *Of Public Wrongs* (Chicago: University of Chicago Press, 1979), 391.

23. 31 USC §§ 3729–3730.

24. Blackstone, *Commentaries,* 4:391–392.

25. Saikrishna B. Prakash, "The Chief Prosecutor," *George Washington Law Review* 73, no. 3 (2005): 521–597.

26. Ex Parte Garland, 71 US 333, 380 (1866).

27. Ex Parte Grossman, 267 US 87, 111, 115 (1925).

28. *Burdick v. United States,* 236 US 79, 94 (1915).

29. *Burdick v. United States.*

30. Habeas Corpus Act, 1679, 31 Car. 2, c. 2, § 12 (Eng.)

31. Act of Settlement, 1701, 12 & 13 Will. 3, c. 2 (Eng.).

32. US Const., art. I, § 2, cl. 5; § 3, cl. 6; art. II, § 4.

33. Congressional Research Service, "Art II. S 4.4.2 Historical Background on Impeachable Offenses," Constitution Annotated, *Constitution of the United States of America: Analysis and Interpretation,* https://constitution.congress.gov/browse/essay/artII-S4-4-2/ALDE_00000699/.

34. Mark Kishlansky, *A Monarchy Transformed: Britain 1603–1714* (New York: Penguin, 1996), 253–255.

35. Kishlansky, *A Monarchy Transformed.*

36. Kishlansky, *A Monarchy Transformed.*

37. David Lindsay Keir, *The Constitutional History of Modern Britain Since 1485* 9th ed. (London: Black, 1969), 256, 258–259.

38. Keir, *Constitutional History of Modern Britain,* 256; Kishlansky, *A Monarchy Transformed,* 304.

39. Act of Settlement, 1701, 12 & 13 Will. 3, c. 2 (Eng.).

40. William F. Duker, "The President's Power to Pardon: A Constitutional History," *William and Mary Law Review* 18, no. 3 (1977): 475–538, 496n109.

41. US Const., art. II, § 2, cl. 1.

42. US Const., art. I, § 3, cl. 7.

43. US Const., art. I, § 2, cl. 5.

44. George Washington, Pardon for Joseph Hood, January 2, 1796, *The Papers of George Washington, Presidential Series,* vol. 19, ed. David R. Hoth (Charlottesville: University of Virginia Press, 2016), 321–322, Founders Online, National Archives, https://founders.archives.gov/documents/Washington/05-19-02-0254.

45. Blackstone, *Commentaries,* 4:393 ("it is a general rule that wherever it may reasonably be presumed the king is deceived, the pardon is void. Therefore any suppression of truth, or suggestion of falsehood, in a charter of pardon will vitiate the whole; for the king was misinformed"); William Hawkins, *A Treatise of the Pleas of the Crown,* vol. 2 (London: Walthoe, 1716), 557 ("if it appears from the recital of a pardon, that the king was misinformed either as to the nature of the case, or

the proceedings thereupon, the pardon is void; as where the king pardons a man for felony whereof he stands indicted . . . and in truth he never was indicted").

46. *Morrison v. Olson,* 487 US 654 (1988), Scalia, J., dissenting.

Chapter 3 · Washingtonian Mercy

1. George Washington to John Adams, May 10, 1789, in *The Papers of George Washington: Presidential Series,* vol. 2, ed. Dorothy Twohig (Charlottesville: University of Virginia Press, 1987), 245, 247–248 (hereafter *Washington Papers, Presidential Series*).

2. George Washington to James Madison, May 5, 1789, in *Washington Papers, Presidential Series,* vol. 2, 216–217.

3. George Washington to Catherine Sawbridge Macaulay Graham, January 9, 1790, in *Washington Papers, Presidential Series,* vol. 4, ed. Dorothy Twohig (1993), 551, 552.

4. See, for example, Edmund Randolph to George Washington, June 25, 1795, in *Washington Papers, Presidential Series,* vol. 18, ed. Carol S. Ebel (2015), 258–259 (Randolph, at the request of the president, weighing in on the Jay Treaty); George Washington to Alexander Hamilton, February 16, 1791, in *Washington Papers, Presidential Series,* vol. 7, ed. Jack D. Warren (1998), 357 (Washington requesting Hamilton's input on the Bank Bill, noting prior input solicited from Jefferson and Randolph); George Washington to Henry Knox, July 22, 1791, in *Washington Papers, Presidential Series,* vol. 8, ed. Mark A. Mastromarino (1993), 370 (Washington asking Henry Knox's opinions on Joseph Habersham, who was a businessman and US postmaster general, appointed 1795, and John Houstoun, who was ex-governor of Georgia and a potential candidate for a US Supreme Court judgeship).

5. See, for example, Thomas Bird to George Washington, June 5, 1790, *Washington Papers, Presidential Series,* vol. 5, ed. Dorothy Twohig, Mark A. Mastromarino, and Jack D. Warren (1996), 478, 479n1 (citing letters to Washington from district judge).

6. See, for example, George Washington to Edmund Randolph, March 1, 1791, in *Washington Papers, Presidential Series,* vol. 7, 493.

7. George Washington to John Jay, June 13, 1790, in *Washington Papers, Presidential Series,* vol. 5, 517.

8. See, for example, George Washington, "Philip Vigol Stay of Execution," June 16, 1795, in *Washington Papers, Presidential Series,* vol. 18, 242–243, Founders Online, National Archives, https://founders.archives.gov/documents/Washington /05-18-02-0181 (reprieves of Philip Vigol [Weigle] and John Mitchell).

9. Jerry Genesio, "The Trial and Execution of Thomas Bird in Portland Maine, 1790: The First Execution under the United States Constitution," *Maine History* 42, no. 4 (2006): 199–214, 208–209.

10. Thomas Bird to George Washington, June 5, 1790, in *Washington Papers, Presidential Series,* vol. 5, 478.

11. Thomas Bird to George Washington, June 5, 1790, 479, note 1, quoting David Sewall to George Washington, June 5, 1790, RG 59, Miscellaneous Letters, 1790–1799, National Archives, excerpts in Founders Online, note 1: https://founders.archives.gov/documents/Washington/05-05-02-0299.

12. George Washington to John Jay, June 13, 1790, in *Washington Papers, Presidential Series,* vol. 5, 517.

13. John Jay to George Washington, June 13, 1790, in *Washington Papers, Presidential Series,* vol. 5, 518.

14. Genesio, "The Trial and Execution of Thomas Bird," 210.

15. Thomas Bird to George Washington, June 5, 1790, 481, note 1, quoting George Washington to David Sewall, June 28, 1790, available at Library of Congress, https://tile.loc.gov/storage-services/service/mss/mgw/mgw2/022/022.pdf, p. 119.

16. George Washington to Edmund Randolph, March 1, 1791, in *Washington Papers, Presidential Series,* vol. 7, 493, and note 1, 493–495.

17. Washington to Edmund Randolph, March 1, 1791, and note 1, 493–495.

18. Washington to Edmund Randolph, March 1, 1791, and note 1, 494, quoting Samuel Dodge's Petition, in RG 59, Miscellaneous Letters, 1790–1799, National Archives; summary in Founders Online, note 1: https://founders.archives.gov/documents/Washington/05-07-02-0273.

19. Washington to Edmund Randolph, March 1, 1791, note 1, 494.

20. Washington to Edmund Randolph, March 1, 1791, 493.

21. Washington to Edmund Randolph, March 1, 1791, note 1, 494–495 (citing Alexander Hamilton to Richard Harrison, April 26, 1791, in *The Papers of Alexander Hamilton,* vol. 8, ed. Harold C. Syrett (New York: Columbia University Press, 2011), 312 (hereafter *Papers of Alexander Hamilton*).

22. *Washington Papers,* vol. 7, 495, note 1 (citing Letter from Richard Harrison to Alexander Hamilton, May 24, 1791, in *Papers of Alexander Hamilton,* vol. 8, 352).

23. Richard Harrison to Alexander Hamilton, May 24, 1791, vol. 8, 352, 353.

24. Tobias Lear to George Washington, October 2, 1791, *Washington Papers, Presidential Series,* vol. 9, ed. Philander D. Chase (2000), 49n1.

25. See Tobias Lear to George Washington, October 2, 1791, 46.

26. Thomas Bird to George Washington, June 5, 1790, 481, note 1, quoting George Washington to David Sewall, June 28, 1790.

27. George Washington to Edmund Randolph, October 10, 1791, in *Washington Papers, Presidential Series,* vol. 9, 68.

28. The description of events draws extensively from William Hogeland, *The Whiskey Rebellion: George Washington, Alexander Hamilton, and the Frontier Rebels*

Who Challenged America's Newfound Sovereignty (New York: Scribner, 2006); and Thomas P. Slaughter, *The Whiskey Rebellion: Frontier Epilogue to the American Revolution* (Oxford: Oxford University Press, 1986).

29. Saikrishna Bangalore Prakash, "Deciphering the Commander in Chief Clause," *Yale Law Journal* 133, no. 1 (2023): 54–55.

30. Lee's proclamation quoted in Alexander Hamilton to William Rawle, November 17–19 1794, in *The Papers of Alexander Hamilton*, vol. 17, 380n14; Hamilton cites *The [New York] Daily Advertiser,* December 6, 1794.

31. Edmund Randolph to George Washington, July 21, 1795, in *Washington Papers, Presidential Series,* vol. 18, 392n4.

32. See the unnumbered note to George Washington, Pardon for Benjamin Parkinson, March 3, 1797, *Washington Papers, Presidential Series,* vol. 21, ed. Adrina Garbooshian-Huggins (2020), 786, Founders Online, https://founders.archives.gov /documents/Washington/05-21-02-0362.

33. George Washington, Philip Vigol Stay of Execution, June 16, 1795.

34. George Washington, John Mitchell Stay of Execution, June 17, 1795, RG 59: General Records of the Department of State, Series: Pardons and Remissions, National Archives and Records Administration, https://catalog.archives.gov/id /423380739?objectPage=9 (hereafter RG 59, NARA).

35. George Washington, Pardon of John Mitchell and Philip Vigol, November 2, 1795, RG 59, NARA, https://catalog.archives.gov/id/423380739?objectPage=9.

36. Bradley D. Hays, "The Politics of Clemency in the Early American Presidency: Power Inherited, Power Refashioned," *Journal of Policy History* 34, no. 1 (2022): 92–115, 100, 102 (claiming that Washington's pardons were political because they advanced particular interests and reflected a "constitutional and political vision").

37. George Washington, Pardon for Ten Additional Whisky Insurgents, March 3, 1797, Gilder Lehrman Institute of American History, GLC08072, https://www .gilderlehrman.org/sites/default/files/GLC/documents/2023-05/GLC08072_OS .docx.pdf.

38. See, for example, George Washington, Pardon for Joseph Agnew, January 4, 1796, RG 59, NARA, https://catalog.archives.gov/id/423380739?objectPage=11.

39. George Washington, Pardon for Munnuckhuysen and Sadler, December 24, 1794, RG 59, entry 690, Petitions for Pardon, NARA; see Charles Peter Carpantier to George Washington, c. December 19–21, 1794, *Washington Papers, Presidential Series,* vol. 17, ed. David R. Hoth and Carol S. Ebel (2013), 292–293, note 4.

40. See, for example, George Washington, Pardon for Joseph Hood, January 2, 1796, *Washington Papers, Presidential Series,* vol. 19, ed. David R. Hoth (2016), 321–322, Founders Online https://founders.archives.gov/documents/Washington /05-19-02-0254 ("fair and honest," "character and conduct"). For both George Washington, Pardon for Robert Gage, September 17, 1796, RG 59, NARA, https://

catalog.archives.gov/id/423380739?objectPage=12 ("fair and honest," "character"); and George Washington, Pardon for Stephen Neilson, March 3, 1797, RG 59, NARA, https://catalog.archives.gov/id/423380739?objectPage=13 ("fair and honest," "character"), see George Washington, Pardon for Benjamin Parkinson, March 3, 1797, *Washington Papers, Presidential Series,* vol. 21, 785–787, footnote, Founders Online, https://founders.archives.gov/documents/Washington/05-21-02-0362.

41. George Washington, Pardon for David Blair, April 15, 1794, RG 59, NARA, https://catalog.archives.gov/id/423380739?objectPage=5; George Washington Presidential Library at Mount Vernon, https://catalog.mountvernon.org/digital /collection/p16829coll27/id/3091/.

42. George Washington to Edmund Randolph, October 10, 1791, in *Washington Papers, Presidential Series,* vol. 9, 68.

43. George Washington, Pardon for William Martin, June 11, 1793, RG 59, NARA, https://catalog.archives.gov/id/423380739?objectPage=6.

44. George Washington, Pardon for Joseph Ravara, Consul for the Republic of Genoa, April 25, 1793, RG 59, NARA, https://catalog.archives.gov/id/423380739 ?objectPage=6,

45. George Washington, Pardon for Thomas Norton, September 20, 1794, RG 59, NARA, https://catalog.archives.gov/id/423380739?objectPage=7.

46. See, for example, George Washington, Pardon for Joseph Hood, January 2, 1796, RG 59, NARA, https://catalog.archives.gov/id/423380739?objectPage=10.

47. See, for example, George Washington, Pardon for Joseph Ravara, Consul for the Republic of Genoa, April 25, 1793, RG 59, NARA, https://catalog.archives.gov/id /423380739?objectPage=6; George Washington, Pardon for John Loughery, June 4, 1795, RG 59, NARA, https://catalog.archives.gov/id/423380739?objectPage=8.

48. Thomas Bird to George Washington, June 5, 1790, 481, note 1, quoting George Washington to David Sewall, June 28, 1790.

49. George Washington to Catherine Sawbridge Macaulay Graham, January 9, 1790.

Chapter 4 · Politics by Other Means

1. George Washington to Catherine Sawbridge Macaulay Graham, January 9, 1790, in *The Papers of George Washington: Presidential Series,* vol. 4, ed. Dorothy Twohig (Charlottesville: University Press of Virginia, 1993), 551–554.

2. Washington to Catherine Sawbridge Macaulay Graham, January 9, 1790.

3. For an absolutely gripping account of these whispers and reason to suppose that they were not mere rumors, see Jack Goldsmith, *In Hoffa's Shadow: A Stepfather, a Disappearance in Detroit, and My Search for the Truth* (New York: Farrar, Straus and Giroux, 2019), 172–177.

4. Paul D. Newman, *Fries's Rebellion: The Enduring Struggle for the American Revolution* (Philadelphia: University of Pennsylvania Press, 2004), ix, 31, 32–33.

5. Newman, *Fries's Rebellion*, ix, 118, 127–131, 140, ch. 5.

6. Newman, *Fries's Rebellion*, 183.

7. Newman, *Fries's Rebellion*, 183.

8. Newman, *Fries's Rebellion*, 184–185.

9. Hamilton, Concerning the Public Conduct and Character of John Adams, [October 24, 1800], in *The Papers of Alexander Hamilton*, vol. 25, *July 1800–April 1802*, ed. Harold C. Syrett (New York: Columbia University Press, 1977), 186–234, 227, Founders Online, National Archives, https://founders.archives.gov/documents /Hamilton/01-25-02-0110-0002.

10. Hamilton, Concerning the Public Conduct and Character of John Adams, [October 24, 1800], 227.

11. Newman, *Fries's Rebellion*, 187.

12. Newman, *Fries's Rebellion*, 185.

13. Alien and Sedition Act of 1798, § 4, 1 Stat. 596 (1798).

14. Saikrishna B. Prakash, "The Chief Prosecutor," *George Washington Law Review* 73, no. 3 (2005): 521–597, 558–559.

15. Prakash, "The Chief Prosecutor," 558–559.

16. Thomas Jefferson to Abigail Adams, July 22, 1804, *The Papers of Thomas Jefferson, Main Series*, vol. 44, *1 July to 10 November 1804*, ed. James P. McClure (Princeton: Princeton University Press, 2019), 129–131 (hereafter *Jefferson Papers*).

17. Thomas Jefferson, Pardon for James Thomson Callender, March 16, 1801, *Jefferson Papers*, vol. 33, ed. Barbara B. Oberg (2006), 309–310; Pardon for David Brown (March 11, 1801), *Jefferson Papers*, vol. 33, 251–252.

18. *The Papers of James Madison, Secretary of State Series*, vol. 1, ed. Robert J. Bruegger (1986), 120n5; US Const. art. I, § 9, cl. 7.

19. James Callender to James Madison, April 27, 1801, in *The Papers of James Madison, Secretary of State Series*, vol. 1, *4 March–31 July 1801*, ed. Robert J. Brugger, Robert A. Rutland, Robert Rhodes Crout, Jeanne K. Sisson, and Dru Dowdy (Charlottesville: University Press of Virginia, 1986), 117–121 (complaining of Jefferson's "ingratitude" and that Jefferson would "sacrifice me as a kind of Scape Goat to political *decorum*").

20. Callender's Case [no date], *Jefferson Papers*, vol. 34, *1 May–31 July 1801*, ed. Robert J. Brugger (1986), 190 note.

21. *The Papers of James Madison, Secretary of State Series*, vol. 1, ed. Robert J. Brugger (1986), 237n4.

22. *Jefferson Papers,* vol. 38, *1 July to 12 November 1802,* ed. Barbara Oberg (2011), 448–449 note (discussing 1802 controversy in the press about Callender's fine, the Attorney General's supposed inconsistency).

23. Annette Gordon-Reed, *Thomas Jefferson and Sally Hemings: An American Controversy* (Charlottesville: University of Virginia Press, 1997), 59–62.

24. Gordon-Reed, *Thomas Jefferson and Sally Hemings,* 59–62, 190.

25. Abigail Adams to Thomas Jefferson, July 1, 1804, in *Jefferson Papers,* vol. 44, 3–6.

26. Jefferson to Abigail Adams, July 22, 1804.

27. Jefferson to Abigail Adams, July 22, 1804.

28. Abigail Adams to Thomas Jefferson, August 18, 1804, *Jefferson Papers,* vol. 44, 243.

29. Jonathan Truman Dorris, *Pardon and Amnesty under Lincoln and Johnson: The Restoration of the Confederates to Their Rights and Privileges, 1861–1898* (Chapel Hill: University of North Carolina Press, 1953), 102–103.

30. Dorris, *Pardon and Amnesty under Lincoln and Johnson,* 35.

31. Act of July 17, 1862, ch. 195, 12 Stat. 589 (1862).

32. Dorris, *Pardon and Amnesty under Lincoln and Johnson,* 325; US Const. art. II, § 2, cl. 1.

33. A Proclamation, December 8, 1863, 13 Stat. 737–739.

34. A Proclamation, December 8, 1863, 13 Stat. 737–739; see also Dorris, *Pardon and Amnesty under Lincoln and Johnson,* 34–35.

35. Dorris, *Pardon and Amnesty under Lincoln and Johnson,* 40–43.

36. Abraham Lincoln to Albert G. Hodges, April 4, 1864, The American Presidency Project, ed. Gerhard Peters and John T. Woolley, University of California, Santa Barbara, https://www.presidency.ucsb.edu/documents/letter-albert-g-hodges (hereafter American Presidency Project).

37. *United States v. Adams,* 2025 WL 978572 No. 24-CR-556 (SDNY filed April 2, 2025).

38. See generally, "The President's Conditional Pardon Power," *Harvard Law Review* 134, no. 8 (2021): 2833–2854; Harold J. Krent, "Conditioning the President's Conditional Pardon Power," *California Law Review* 89, no. 6 (2001): 1665–1720.

39. A Proclamation, May 29, 1865, in 13 Stat. 758–760.

40. Dorris, *Pardon and Amnesty under Lincoln and Johnson,* 314, 111, 112, 221.

41. Dorris, *Pardon and Amnesty under Lincoln and Johnson,* 116, 126–127, 350–351, 325, 415–416.

42. A Proclamation, September 7, 1867, in 15 Stat. 699–700.

43. Dorris, *Pardon and Amnesty under Lincoln and Johnson,* 343.

44. Dorris, *Pardon and Amnesty under Lincoln and Johnson,* 343–345.

45. Dorris, *Pardon and Amnesty under Lincoln and Johnson,* 351–354.

46. A Proclamation, September 7, 1867, in 15 Stat. 699–700.

47. Dorris, *Pardon and Amnesty under Lincoln and Johnson,* 355.

48. Dorris, *Pardon and Amnesty under Lincoln and Johnson,* 357.

49. A Proclamation, September 7, 1867, in 15 Stat. 699–700.

50. Dorris, *Pardon and Amnesty under Lincoln and Johnson,* 358–359.

51. Paul H. Bergeron, *Andrew Johnson's Civil War and Reconstruction* (Knoxville: University of Tennessee Press, 2011), 210.

52. Bergeron, *Andrew Johnson's Civil War and Reconstruction,* 211.

53. Brian C. Kalt, "Pardon Me? The Constitutional Case Against Presidential Self-Pardons," *Yale Law Journal* 106, no. 3 (1996): 779–809, 779, 800.

54. Proclamation Bo. 4311, 39 Fed. Reg. 32, 601–602 (September 8, 1974).

55. Gerald R. Ford, "Proclamation no. 4311—Granting Pardon to Richard Nixon," 39 Fed. Reg. 32, 601–602, 32,602 (September 8, 1974), American Presidency Project, https://www.presidency.ucsb.edu/documents/proclamation-4311-granting-pardon -richard-nixon.

56. Stephen F. Knott, *The Lost Soul of the American Presidency: The Decline into Demagoguery and the Prospects for Renewal* (Lawrence, KS: University Press of Kansas, 2020), 185.

57. Jeffrey Toobin, *The Pardon: The Politics of Presidential Mercy* (New York: Simon and Schuster, 2025), 207.

58. Harold M. Schmeck Jr., "Reaction to Pardon of Nixon Is Divided, But Not Entirely Along Party Lines," *New York Times,* September 9, 1974.

59. Schmeck Jr., "Reaction to Pardon of Nixon Is Divided."

60. "The Failure of Mr. Ford," *New York Times,* September 9, 1974.

61. Clifton Daniel, "Ford's Gallup Rating Off 21 Points after Pardon," *New York Times,* October 13, 1974.

62. Edward M. Kennedy, "Remarks on Presenting the 2001 Profile in Courage Award to President Gerald R. Ford and the Lifetime Achievement Award to Congressman John Lewis," May 21, 2001, John F. Kennedy Library and Museum, Boston, MA, https://www.jfklibrary.org/events-and-awards/profile-in-courage-award/award -recipients/john-lewis-2001.

63. Toobin, *The Pardon,* 212–213, 256.

64. George Bush, "Proclamation No. 6518—Grant of Executive Clemency," 57 Fed. Reg. 62,145 December 24, 1992, American Presidency Project, https://www .presidency.ucsb.edu/documents/proclamation-6518-grant-executive-clemency.

65. "Lawrence E. Walsh Dies at 102: Iran-Contra Independent Prosecutor," *Los Angeles Times,* March 20, 2014.

66. Ronald J. Ostrow and Robert L. Jackson, "Pardon by Bush Conceals Facts, Walsh Asserts," *Los Angeles Times,* February 9, 1993.

67. David Johnston, "Bush Pardons 6 in Iran Affair, Aborting a Weinberger Trial," *New York Times,* December 25, 1992.

68. Dan Morgan and David S. Broder, "President to Disclose 'Everything': White House Disputes Walsh's Charges of Iran-Contra Coverup," *Washington Post,* December 25, 1992

69. "Hillary Rodham Clinton's New York Senate Campaign (1999–2001)," William J. Clinton Presidential Library & Museum, Presidential Pardons, https://clinton.presidentiallibraries.us/collections/show/70.

70. Robert Waddell, "Latino Vote Takes Hillary to New York Senate Victory," *Puerto Rico Herald,* November 8, 2000.

71. Katharine Q. Seelye, "Clinton to Commute Radicals' Sentences," *New York Times,* August 12, 1999.

72. "Clemency for FALN Members," Senate Hearing 106–799: Hearings before the Committee on the Judiciary, United States Senate, 106th Congress, First Session, on Examining Certain Implications of the President's Grant of Clemency for Members of the Armed Forces on National Liberation (the FALN), September 15, and October 20, 1999 (Washington, DC: US Government Publishing Office, 2000), https://www.govinfo.gov/content/pkg/CHRG-106shrg68017/html/CHRG-106shrg68017.htm.

73. John King, Jonathan Aiken, and Bill Mears, "White House Responds to Criticisms of Clemency Offer, *CNN,* September 2, 1999, http://www.cnn.com/ALLPOLITICS/stories/1999/09/02/clemency/.

74. Chris Black, First Lady Opposes Presidential Clemency for Puerto Rican Nationalists, *CNN,* September 5, 1999, https://www.cnn.com/ALLPOLITICS/stories/1999/09/05/senate.2000/hillary.puerto.rico/.

75. 145 Cong. Rec. H8012–13 (daily ed. September 9, 1999); 156 Cong. Rec. S10818 (daily ed. September 14, 1999).

76. Terry Frieden, "Justice Blocks FBI Testimony at FALN Clemency Hearing," *CNN,* September 14, 1999, https://web.archive.org/web/20041212160357/http://cgi.cnn.com/US/9909/14/fbi.faln/.

77. Sonya Ross, "Clinton Pardons More Than 100," *Washington Post,* January 20, 2001.

78. Nick Anderson, "Hasidic Clemency Case Entangles Hillary Clinton," *Los Angeles Times,* February 24, 2001.

79. Eric N. Berg, "Marc Rich Indicted in Vast Tax Evasion Case," *New York Times,* September 20, 1983.

80. "Denise Rich Gave $450,000 to Clinton Library," *ABC News,* February 9, 2001, https://abcnews.go.com/Politics/story?id=121846&page=1.

81. David Stout, "Senate Panel Opens Hearing on Rich Pardon," *New York Times,* February 14, 2001.

82. Jonah Goldberg, "The Clintons Lower the Bar—Again," *Los Angeles Times,* April 29, 2015.

83. "Carter Calls Pardon of Rich 'Disgraceful,'" *Los Angeles Times,* February 21, 2001.

84. Jefferson to Abigail Adams, July 22, 1804.

85. Jefferson to Abigail Adams, July 22, 1804.

Chapter 5 · A Tale of Two Clemencies

1. Ken Belson and Eric Lichtblau, "A Father, A Son, and A Short-Lived Presidential Pardon," *New York Times,* December 25, 2008.

2. Belson and Lichtblau, "A Father, A Son."

3. Donald J. Trump, "Executive Grant of Clemency, Charles Kushner," December 23, 2020, https://www.justice.gov/pardon/media/1112541/dl?inline.

4. Donald J. Trump, "Executive Grant of Clemency, Joseph M. Arpaio," August 25, 2017, https://www.justice.gov/pardon/file/993586/dl?inline.

5. Donald J. Trump, "Executive Grant of Clemency, Michael T. Flynn," November 25, 2020, https://www.justice.gov/pardon/page/file/1341606/dl?inline; Donald J. Trump, "Executive Grant of Clemency, Roger Jason Stone Jr.," December 23, 2020, https://www.justice.gov/pardon/media/1112531/dl?inline; Donald J. Trump, "Executive Grant of Clemency, Paul J. Manafort Jr.," December 23, 2020, https://www.justice.gov/pardon/media/1112506/dl?inline.

6. U.S. Const. amend. XX, § 1, cl. 1.

7. Michelle Stoddart and Lucien Bruggeman, "President Biden Pardons Family Members in Final Minutes of Presidency," *ABC News,* January 20, 2025, https://abcnews.go.com/Politics/president-biden-pardons-family-members-final-minutes-presidency/story?id=117893348.

8. Joseph R. Biden Jr., "Executive Grant of Clemency, James B. Biden, Sara Jones Biden, Valerie Biden Owens, John T. Owens, and Francis W. Biden," January 19, 2025, https://www.justice.gov/pardon/media/1385756/dl?inline.

9. Joseph R. Biden Jr., "Executive Grant of Clemency, Robert Hunter Biden," December 1, 2024, https://www.justice.gov/pardon/media/1378646/dl?inline. Compare its wording ("For those offenses") with that of Biden Jr., "Executive Grant of Clemency, James B. Biden, Sara Jones Biden, Valerie Biden Owens, John T. Owens, and Francis W. Biden" ("For any nonviolent offenses").

10. Tamara Keith, "Biden Pardons Fauci, Milley and Members of Jan. 6 Panel," *NPR,* January 20, 2025, https://www.npr.org/2025/01/20/nx-s1-5268258/biden-pardons-fauci-milley-and-members-of-jan-6-panel.

11. Kevin Liptak and Arlette Saenz, "Biden Issues Preemptive Pardons for Trump Critics and Biden Family Members," *CNN,* January 20, 2025, https://www.cnn.com/2025/01/20/politics/joe-biden-preemptive-pardons.

12. Donald J. Trump, "Granting Pardons and Commutation of Sentences for Certain Offenses Relating to the Events at or Near the United States Capitol on January 6, 2021," Proclamation No. 10887, 90 Fed. Reg. 8331, January 20, 2025, https://www.federalregister.gov/documents/2025/01/29/2025-01950/granting -pardons-and-commutation-of-sentences-for-certain-offenses-relating-to-the -events-at-or-near.

13. Tim Reid, "Trump Cites Supreme Court Ruling in Calling for Jan. 6 'Hostages' to Be Freed," Reuters June 28, 2024, https://www.reuters.com/world/us /trump-cites-supreme-court-ruling-calling-jan-6-hostages-be-freed-2024-06-28/.

14. Trump, "Granting Pardons and Commutation of Sentences for Certain Offenses Relating to the Events at or Near the United States Capitol on January 6, 2021," Proclamation No. 10887.

15. See, for example, Andrew Stanton, "Democratic Attorney Blasts 'Phony' Donald Trump Charges in New York," *Newsweek,* April 25, 2024, https://www .newsweek.com/democratic-attorney-blasts-donald-trump-charges-1894221.

16. Jon Levine, "Disgraced ex-Gov. Andrew Cuomo Blasts Alvin Bragg's Probe of Trump," *New York Post,* March 25, 2023.

17. David Smith, "'I Am Your Retribution': Trump Rules Supreme at CPAC as He Relaunches Bid for White House," *The Guardian,* March 4, 2023.

18. Donald J. Trump (@realDonaldTrump), TruthSocial, September 22, 2023, 19:59 ET, https://truthsocial.com/@realDonaldTrump/posts/111111513207332826. Whether Trump was referring to a Milley phone call to Chinese officials post–January 6, 2025, or a Milley phone conversation from 2024 is a bit uncertain.

19. Donald Trump, interviewed by Kristen Welker, *Meet the Press,* NBC News, December 8, 2024, quote at 26.58, https://www.youtube.com/watch?v=-UsHJWEAj_I.

20. Elon Musk (@elonmusk), X, December 11, 2022, 05:58 ET, https://x.com /elonmusk/status/1601894132573605888?lang=en.

21. Ted Cruz (@tedcruz), X, December 5, 2022, 23:11 ET, https://x.com/tedcruz /status/1599981205318934529.

22. Martin Pengelly, "Mark Milley Fears Being Court-Martialed If Trump Wins, Woodward Book Says," *The Guardian,* October 11, 2024; Brett Samuels, "Trump Calls for Jan. 6 Committee to Be Indicted," *The Hill,* June 6, 2024, https://thehill .com/homenews/campaign/4708462-trump-jan-6-committee-members-indicted -bannon/; Vaughn Hillyard, David Rohde and Ken Dilanian, "Trump Is Increasingly Vowing to Prosecute Political Foes and Others He Says Are 'Corrupt' If He Wins," *NBC News,* September 9, 2024, https://www.nbcnews.com/investigations/trump -vows-prosecute-political-foes-others-corrupt-cheaters-rcna169292.

23. Joseph R. Biden Jr., "Executive Grant of Clemency, Members of Congress Who Served on the Select Committee to Investigate the January 6th Attack on the United States Capitol," January 19, 2025, https://www.justice.gov/pardon/media

/1385751/dl?inline; Joseph R. Biden Jr., "Executive Grant of Clemency, Mark A. Milley," January 19, 2025, https://www.justice.gov/pardon/media/1385741/dl?inline; Joseph R. Biden Jr., "Executive Grant of Clemency, Anthony S. Fauci," January 19, 2025, https://www.justice.gov/pardon/media/1385746/dl?inline.

24. Zachary Cohen and Kara Scannell, "Former Business Partner Says Hunter Biden Sold 'Illusion' of Access to Joe Biden, Source Says," *CNN,* July 31, 2023, https://www.cnn.com/2023/07/31/politics/devon-archer-house-testimony.

25. Ben Schreckinger, "Biden Insists He's Not Involved in His Family's Business Dealings. But His Aides Are a Different Story," *Politico,* June 8, 2024, https://www.politico.com/news/2024/06/08/joe-biden-aides-family-business-dealings-00161476.

26. Josh Lederman, "Biden's Trip to China with Son Hunter in 2013 Comes Under New Scrutiny," *NBC News,* October 2, 2019, https://www.nbcnews.com/politics/2020-election/biden-s-trip-china-son-hunter-2013-comes-under-new-n1061051.

27. Matt Viser, "Hunter Biden's Career of Benefiting from His Father's Name," *Washington Post,* November 18, 2023.

28. Luke Broadwater, "House Republicans Issue Criminal Referrals of Hunter and James Biden," *New York Times,* June 5, 2024.

29. Glenn Kessler, "How Republicans Overhype the Findings of Their Hunter Biden Probe," *Washington Post,* August 23, 2023.

30. Viser, "Hunter Biden's Career of Benefiting."; Schreckinger, "Biden Said His Pardon of His Family Was Meant to Shield Them from Trump: That's Not the Full Story," *Politico,* January 20, 2025, https://www.politico.com/news/2025/01/20/joe-biden-family-pardon-jim-00199370.

31. Viser, "Hunter Biden's Career of Benefiting."

32. Viser, "Hunter Biden's Career of Benefiting."

33. Schreckinger, "Biden Said His Pardon of His Family Was Meant to Shield Them from Trump."

34. Michael Shear and Zolan Kanno-Youngs, "Biden Issues a 'Full and Unconditional Pardon' of His Son Hunter Biden," *New York Times,* December 1, 2024.

35. Biden Jr., "Executive Grant of Clemency, Robert Hunter Biden," December 1, 2024.

36. Shear and Kanno-Youngs, "Biden Issues a 'Full and Unconditional Pardon' of His Son Hunter Biden."

37. Jake Horton and Matt Murphy, "What Has Joe Biden Said in the Past About Pardoning His Son?" *BBC,* December 2, 2024, https://www.bbc.com/news/articles/ceql5v5voxlo

38. Horton and Murphy, "What Has Joe Biden Said in the Past About Pardoning His Son?"

39. Biden Jr., "Executive Grant of Clemency, Robert Hunter Biden," December 1, 2024.

40. Betsy Woodruff Swan, "We Haven't Seen a Pardon as Sweeping as Hunter Biden's in Generations," *Politico,* December 2, 2024, https://www.politico.com/news /2024/12/02/hunter-biden-pardon-nixon-00192101.

41. Swan, "We Haven't Seen a Pardon as Sweeping as Hunter Biden's in Generations."

42. Swan, "We Haven't Seen a Pardon as Sweeping as Hunter Biden's in Generations."

43. Shear and Kanno-Youngs, "Biden Issues a 'Full and Unconditional Pardon' of His Son Hunter Biden."

44. Carol Lee and Sarah Fitzpatrick, "President Biden Pardons His Son Hunter Biden," *NBC News,* December 21, 2024, https://www.nbcnews.com/politics/joe -biden/joe-biden-issue-pardon-son-hunter-biden-rcna182369.

45. Joseph R. Biden Jr., "Executive Grant of Clemency, James B. Biden, Sara Jones Biden, Valerie Biden Owens, John T. Owens, Francis W. Biden," January 19, 2025.

46. Biden Jr., "Executive Grant of Clemency, James B. Biden, Sara Jones Biden, Valerie Biden Owens, John T. Owens, Francis W. Biden."

47. Biden Jr., "Executive Grant of Clemency, James B. Biden, Sara Jones Biden, Valerie Biden Owens, John T. Owens, Francis W. Biden" ("For any nonviolent offenses . . .").

48. Joseph R. Biden Jr., "Presidential Statement on Pardon of James Biden, Sara Jones Biden, Valerie Biden Owens, John T. Owens, and Francis W. Biden," January 20, 2025, https://bidenwhitehouse.archives.gov/briefing-room/statements -releases/2025/01/20/statement-from-president-joe-biden-16/.

49. Biden Jr., "Presidential Statement on Pardon."

50. See, for example, James Comer, "Biden Family Pardons a Confession to Selling Out America," *Fox News,* January 25, 2025, https://www.foxnews.com /opinion/rep-james-comer-biden-crime-family-pardons-were-just-cover-up-30 -million-dirty-deeds.

51. Schreckinger, "Biden Said His Pardon of His Family Was Meant to Shield Them From Trump."

52. Arizona Representative Andy Biggs, quoted in Megan Lebowitz, "Republicans Fume after Biden Pardons His Son Hunter," *NBC News,* December 1, 2024, https://www.nbcnews.com/politics/white-house/congressional-reaction-president -joe-biden-pardons-hunter-rcna182375.

53. Arkansas Senator Tom Cotton, quoted in Lebowitz, "Republicans Fume."

54. Colorado Governor Jared Polis, quoted in Lebowitz, "Republicans Fume."

55. Connecticut Senator Richard Blumenthal, quoted in Helen Huiskes and Em Luetkemeyer, "Democrats Say Blanket Pardons for Biden's Family Is Terrible Precedent," *NOTUS,* January 20, 2025, https://www.notus.org/whitehouse/democrats -pardons-biden-precedent.

56. Colorado Senator Michael Bennet, quoted in Alexander Bolton, "Democratic Senator Blasts Biden's Pardon of Son," *The Hill,* December 2, 2024, https://thehill .com/homenews/senate/5017720-biden-grants-hunter-pardon/.

57. Jordyn Phelps and Ben Gittleson, "Trump Still in Denial About Defeat as Legal Team Mounts Last-Ditch Challenges," *ABC News,* November 30, 2020, https://abcnews.go.com/Politics/trump-denial-defeat-legal-team-mounts-ditch -challenges/story?id=74461744.

58. Ann Gerhart, "Election Results Under Attack: Here Are the Facts," *Washington Post: Elections,* December 9, 2020.

59. Caroline Linton, "All 538 Electors Have Voted, Formalizing Biden's 306–232 Win. Here's How the Electoral College Works," *CBS News,* December 15, 2020, https://www.cbsnews.com/news/electoral-college-votes-joe-biden-victory/.

60. Brian Naylor, "Trump Calls on Pence to Reject Electoral Votes. Pence Says He Won't," *NPR,* January 6, 2021, https://www.npr.org/sections/congress-electoral -college-tally-live-updates/2021/01/06/953998465/trump-calls-on-pence-to-reject -electoral-votes-pence-says-he-wont.

61. Brian Naylor, "Read Trump's Jan. 6 Speech, A Key Part of Impeachment Trial," *NPR,* February 10, 2021, https://www.npr.org/2021/02/10/966396848/read -trumps-jan-6-speech-a-key-part-of-impeachment-trial. Video of speech embedded: "Fight like hell" quote at 1:51.

62. Bob Woodward and Robert Costa, "Jan. 6 White House Logs Given to House Show 7-Hour Gap in Trump Calls," *Washington Post,* March 29, 2022.

63. Woodward and Costa, "Jan. 6 White House Logs."

64. Chris Cameron, "These Are the People Who Died in Connection with the Capitol Riot," *New York Times,* January 5, 2022.

65. Naylor, "Read Trump's Jan. 6 Speech, A Key Part of Impeachment Trial."

66. Naylor, "Read Trump's Jan. 6 Speech, A Key Part of Impeachment Trial."

67. Valentino-DeVries, Grace Ashford, Denise Lu, Eleanor Denise, Alex Leeds Matthews, and Karen Yourish, "Arrested in Capitol Riot: Organized Militants and a Horde of Radicals," *New York Times,* February 4, 2021.

68. Ryan J. Reilly, "Trump Pardons over 1500 Criminal Defendants Charged in the Jan. 6 Capitol Attack," *NBC News,* January 20, 2025, https://www.nbcnews .com/politics/justice-department/trump-set-pardon-defendants-stormed-capitol -jan-6-2021-rcna187735.

69. Pamela Brown, Kevin Liptak, and Katelyn Polantz, "Trump Announces Wave of Pardons, Including Papadopoulos and Former Lawmakers Hunter and Col-

lins," *CNN Politics,* December 23, 2020, https://www.cnn.com/2020/12/22/politics/trump-pardons.

70. Eric Cortellessa, "How Far Trump Would Go," *Time,* April 30, 2024.

71. David Klepper, "Music to Trump's Ears: Whitewashing Jan. 6 Riot with Song," *AP News,* April 21, 2023, https://apnews.com/article/j6-choir-trump-national-anthem-capitol-riot-79618f1f2a689c308dfdc34d54d327ea.

72. Issac Arnsdorf, Meg Kelly, Rachel Weiner, and Tom Jackman, "Behind Trump's Musical Tribute to Some of the Most Violent Jan 6 Rioters," *Washington Post,* May 7, 2023; Marianne LeVine et al., "Trump Escalates Solidarity with Jan. 6 Rioters as His Own Trials Close In," *Washington Post,* March 23, 2024.

73. Cortellessa, "How Far Trump Would Go."

74. Leila Fadel and Obed Manuel, "Trump Said He Would Pardon Jan. 6 Rioters. How Does that Power Work?" *NPR,* November 13, 2024, https://www.npr.org/2024/11/11/nx-s1-5181960/can-trump-pardon-as-promised-people-convicted-in-connection-with-the-jan-6-attack.

75. Marshall Cohen, Donie O'Sullivan, and Curt Devine, "'He Has to Deliver': Trump's Dilemma on How Far to Go with Promised Pardons for January 6 Rioters," *CNN Politics,* November 12, 2024, https://www.cnn.com/2024/11/12/politics/trump-january-6-rioters-pardons.

76. Cohen, O'Sullivan, and Devine, "'He Has to Deliver.'"

77. Cohen, O'Sullivan, and Devine, "'He Has to Deliver.'"

78. Taylor Penley, "JD Vance Spells Out What Trump's Process to 'Rectify' 'Unfair' Jan 6 Prosecutions Could Look Like," *Fox News,* January 12, 2025, https://www.foxnews.com/media/jd-vance-trump-process-rectify-unfair-jan-6-prosecutions.

79. Bart Jansen, Savannah Kuchar, and Sudiksha Kochi, "Donald Trump's Pledge of 'Major Pardons' for Jan. 6 Defendants Has Allies, Critics on Edge," *USA Today,* January 17, 2025.

80. Trump, "Granting Pardons and Commutation of Sentences for Certain Offenses Relating to the Events at or Near the United States Capitol on January 6, 2021," Proclamation No. 10887.

81. Alexandra Marquez, "Sen. Lindsey Graham Says He Thinks Trump Pardoning Violent Jan. 6 Defendants Was 'A Mistake,'" *NBC News,* January 26, 2025, https://www.nbcnews.com/politics/donald-trump/lindsey-graham-trump-pardoning-violent-jan-6-defendant-mistake-rcna189322.

82. Scott Wong, Frank Thorp V, Kate Santaliz, and Katie Taylor, "'I Just Can't Agree': Trump's Jan. 6 Pardons Face Pushback from Some Republican Senators," *NBC News,* January 21, 2025, https://www.nbcnews.com/politics/congress/trump-jan-6-pardons-pushback-republican-senators-rcna188609.

83. Wong et al., "'I Just Can't Agree.'"

84. Wong et al., "'I Just Can't Agree.'"

85. "President Donald Trump Explains Pardoning January 6 Defendants," *Fox News,* January 22, 2025, https://www.foxnews.com/video/6367536545112, at 3:14.

86. David Smith, "'Very Minor Incidents': Trump Defends January 6 Pardons in Hannity Interview," *The Guardian,* January 23, 2025.

87. Smith, "'Very Minor Incidents.'"

88. Marc Caputo, "'F—k It: Release 'Em All': Why Trump Embraced Broad Jan. 6 Pardons," *Axios,* January 22, 2025, https://www.axios.com/2025/01/22/trump-pardons-jan6-clemency.

89. Tom Dreisbach, "Criminal Records of Jan. 6 Rioters Pardoned by Trump Include Rape, Domestic Violence," *NPR,* January. 30, 2025, https://www.npr.org/2025/01/30/nx-s1-5276336/donald-trump-jan-6-rape-assault-pardons-rioters.

90. Tom Jackman, "Some Judges Reject DOJ Claim That Jan. 6 Pardons Apply to Other Crimes," *Washington Post,* May 27, 2025.

91. Trump, "Granting Pardons and Commutation of Sentences for Certain Offenses Relating to the Events at or Near the United States Capitol on January 6, 2021," Proclamation No. 10887.

92. Kyle Cheney, "DOJ Has Abruptly Broadened Its View of Trump's Jan. 6 Pardons. A Judge Wants Answers," *Politico,* February 26, 2025, https://www.politico.com/news/2025/02/26/trump-january-6-pardon-judge-00206301.

93. *United States v. Wilson,* Nos. 25-cv-545, 23-cr-427, 2025 WL 1009047, at *4 (DDC March 13, 2025), (holding that, for an offense to fall within the scope of the pardon, "it must be tethered to a specific time—January 6, 2021—and place—at or near the U.S. Capitol").

94. *United States v. Wilson,* No. 25-3041, 2025 WL 999985, at *2 DC Cir. Apr. 2, 2025.

95. *United States v. Wilson,* No. 25-3041, 2025 WL 999985, at 2–3 (Rao, J., dissenting).

96. Jackman, "Some Judges Reject DOJ Claim" (noting that some judges accept DOJ claim).

97. Trump, "Granting Pardons and Commutation of Sentences for Certain Offenses Relating to the Events at or Near the United States Capitol on January 6, 2021," Proclamation No. 10887.

98. Eric Tucker, "Pardons by Trump and Biden Reveal Distrust of Each Other and Wobbly Faith in Criminal Justice System," *PBS News,* January 22, 2025, https://www.pbs.org/newshour/politics/pardons-by-trump-and-biden-reveal-distrust-of-each-other-and-wobbly-faith-in-criminal-justice-system.

99. Wong et al., "'I Just Can't Agree.'"

Chapter 6 · Our Pardon Dystopia

1. Office of the Pardon Attorney, U.S. Department of Justice, "Clemency Statistics," updated January 23, 2025, https://www.justice.gov/pardon/clemency-statistics (hereafter Office of the Pardon Attorney).January

2. Office of the Pardon Attorney, "Frequently Asked Questions," updated June 16, 2025, https://www.justice.gov/pardon/frequently-asked-questions.

3. Office of the Pardon Attorney, "Frequently Asked Questions."

4. U.S. Department of Justice, Justice Manual § 9–140.112 (2018).

5. Justice Manual § 9–140.113 (2018).

6. Justice Manual § 9–140.112 (2018).

7. Justice Manual § 9–140.113 (2018).

8. Justice Manual § 9–140.111 (2018).

9. Justice Manual § 9–140.110 (2018).

10. Zolan Kanno-Youngs, "Biden Uses Clemency Powers for the First Time," *New York Times,* April 26, 2022.

11. Beth Reinhard, Ann E. Marimow, and Perry Stein, "Biden Pardoned Son while Leaving Hundreds Seeking Clemency in Limbo," *Washington Post,* December 22, 2024.

12. Office of the Pardon Attorney, "Frequently Asked Questions."

13. Matthew Gluck and Jack Goldsmith, "Donald Trump and the Clemency Process," *Federal Sentencing Reporter* 33, no. 5 (2021): 297–300, 299.

14. Gluck and Goldsmith, "Donald Trump and the Clemency Process," 299.

15. C. Ryan Barber, Annie Linskey, and Sadie Gurman, "Biden Commutations Angered His Own Justice Department," *Wall Street Journal,* February 2, 2025.

16. Barber, Linskey, and Gurman, "Biden Commutations Angered His Own Justice Department"; Emily Davies and Perry Stein, "What It Takes to Get a Trump Pardon: Loyalty, Connections or the Pardon Czar," *Washington Post,* June 11, 2025.

17. "Carter: Rich Pardon 'Disgraceful,'" *CBS News,* February 21, 2001, https://www.cbsnews.com/news/carter-rich-pardon-disgraceful/.

18. Barber, Linskey, and Gurman, "Biden Commutations Angered His Own Justice Department."

19. Devlin Barrett, "Justice Dept. Official Says She Was Fired after Opposing Restoring Mel Gibson's Gun Rights," *New York Times,* March 10, 2025.

20. Chandelis Duster, "Who Is Alice Marie Johnson, Trump's Newly Appointed 'Pardon Czar'?" *NPR,* February 25, 2025, https://www.npr.org/2025/02/25/nx-s1-5307330/trump-pardon-czar-who-is-alice-marie-johnson.

21. See Duster, "Who Is Alice Marie Johnson"; Jeff Mason, "Trump Pardons Alice Johnson, Whose Cause Was Backed by Kim Kardashian," Reuters August 28, 2020,

https://www.reuters.com/article/world/trump-pardons-alice-johnson-whose-cause
-was-backed-by-kim-kardashian-idUSKBN25O2R2/.

22. See K. J. Kesselring, *Mercy and Authority in the Tudor State* (Cambridge: Cambridge University Press, 2003), 125–128 (discussing various pardon "intercessors" and gifts and douceurs for intercessors and court patrons); Peter King, *Crime, Justice, and Discretion in England, 1740–1820* (New York: Oxford University Press, 2000), 318–319 ("Although prisoners with aristocratic support were only slightly more successful in gaining a positive recommendation from the judge, they had a much greater chance of over-riding him when he did not report in their favour").

23. Jonathan Dorris, *Pardon and Amnesty under Lincoln and Johnson* (Chapel Hill: University of North Carolina Press, 1953), 144.

24. Dorris, *Pardon and Amnesty under Lincoln and Johnson,* 146.

25. Dorris, *Pardon and Amnesty under Lincoln and Johnson,* 146, (quoting Attorney General's Office to Hon. F. H. Pierpont, Governor of Virginia, August 27, 1865; *New York Herald* September 2, 1865).

26. Ava Benny-Morrison and Bill Allison, "Lawyers Are Quoting $1 Million in Fees to Get Pardons to Trump," *Bloomberg,* May 6, 2025, https://www.bloomberg .com/news/features/2025-05-06/trump-s-pardons-have-defendants-spending-1 -million-to-get-cases-to-white-house; Eliza Collins, Rebecca Ballhaus, and Corinne Ramey, "The Wild West of Presidential Pardons in Trump's Second Term," *Wall Street Journal,* May 12, 2025.

27. Benny-Morrison and Allison, "Lawyers Are Quoting $1 Million in Fees"; Collins, Ballhaus, and Ramey, "The Wild West of Presidential Pardons in Trump's Second Term."

28. Jim Henry, "How FSU Legend Deion Sanders Helped Secure a Pardon from Donald Trump for Rapper Lil Wayne," *Tallahassee Democrat,* January 20, 2021, https://www.tallahassee.com/story/sports/2021/01/20/pardon-lil-wayne-donald -trump-president-deion-sanders-fsu-presidential-rapper-list/4227164001/; Jeff Mason, "Trump Pardons Alice Johnson."

29. Mark Osler, "The Trump Clemencies: Celebrities, Chaos, and Lost Opportunity," *William and Mary Bill of Rights Journal* 31, no. 2 (2022): 487–517, 510.

30. Mark Osler, "It's Time to Stop Pardoning Turkeys," *Wall Street Journal,* November 21, 2019.

31. Osler, "The Trump Clemencies," 510–511.

32. Benny-Morrison and Allison, "Lawyers Are Quoting $1 Million in Fees."

33. Office of the Pardon Attorney, "Executive Grant of Clemency of HDR Global Trading Limited," press release, March 27, 2025, https://www.justice.gov/pardon /media/1394996/dl?inline; Office of the Pardon Attorney, "Executive Grant of

Clemency of Ozy Media, Inc.," press release, March 28, 2025, https://www.justice
.gov/pardon/media/1394996/dl?inline.

34. Minute Entry, *United States v. HDR Glob. Trading Ltd.*, No. 1:24-cr-00424
(SDNY January 15, 2025).

35. *United States v. Watson*, No. 1:23-cr-00082, EDNY, February 16, 2025.

36. For a general discussion of pardoning corporations, see Brandon Stras,
"Pardoning Corporations," *University of Chicago Law Review* 92 (forthcoming).

37. Stras, "Pardoning Corporations."

38. U.S. House Committee on the Judiciary, 119th Congress, "President Trump's
Pardons Cheat Victims Out of an Astounding $1.3 Billion in Restitution and Fines,
Allowing Fraudsters, Tax Evaders, Drug Traffickers to Keep Ill-Gotten Gains,"
Memo, June 17, 2025, https://democrats-judiciary.house.gov/sites/evo-subsites
/democrats-judiciary.house.gov/files/evo-media-document/2025-06-17.dem-memo
-re-%241.3b-cost-of-trump-pardons.pdf.

39. See, for example, Jeevna Sheth, "*Trump v. United States:* A Foundation for
Authoritarian Actions an American President Can Now Commit with Impunity,"
Center for American Progress, August 7, 2024, https://www.americanprogress
.org/article/trump-v-united-states-a-foundation-for-authoritarian-actions-an
-american-president-can-now-commit-with-impunity; Sean O'Driscoll, "Donald
Trump Could Sell Pardons Under New Immunity Ruling—Legal Analyst," *Newsweek,* July 4, 2024.

40. Trump v. United States, 603 U.S. 593, 608 (2024).

41. 603 U.S. 593, 634, 655 (Barrett, J., concurring).

42. James V. Grimaldi, "Denise Rich Gave Clinton Library $450,000," *Washington
Post,* February 9, 2001.

43. "Carter: Rich Pardon 'Disgraceful,'" *CBS News,* February 21, 2001, https://www
.cbsnews.com/news/carter-rich-pardon-disgraceful/.

44. Benny-Morrison and Allison, "Lawyers Are Quoting $1 Million."

45. "Nikola Founder Says $2 Million in Political Donations to Trump Had
Nothing to Do with Pardon," 12News KPNX [NBC Mesa-Phoenix], March 31, 2025,
https://www.youtube.com/watch?v=ZaVljobcyS4&ab_channel=12News.

46. Michael S. Schmidt and Kenneth P. Vogel, "Prospect of Pardons in Final
Days Fuels Market to Buy Access to Trump," *New York Times,* January 17, 2021.

47. See, for example, Kevin Grier, Robin Grier, and Gor Mkrtchian, "Campaign
Contributions and Roll-Call Voting in the U.S. House of Representatives: The
Case of the Sugar Industry," *American Political Science Review* 117, no. 1 (2023):
340–346.

48. See, for example, Michael Beckel, "Big Donors and Bundlers Among Obama's
Ambassador Picks," *OpenSecrets,* May 28, 2009, https://www.opensecrets.org/news
/2009/05/big-donors-bundlers-among-obam.html.

49. See Andrew Ingram, "Dresser Drawer Pardons: Presidential Pardons as Private Acts," *George Mason Law Review* 30 (2023): 721–762, 746–747 (arguing that oral pardons are likely invalid).

50. See, for example, David Loades, *Two Tudor Conspiracies* (Cambridge: Cambridge University Press, 1965), 116, 117 (describing Queen Mary's oral pardons issued on the streets).

51. *Rosemond v. Hudgins*, 92 F.4th 518, 521, 522, 526, 529 (2024).

52. Office of the Pardon Attorney, "President George W. Bush Grants Pardons and Commutation," US Department of Justice, December 23, 2008, https://www.justice.gov/archive/opa/pr/2008/December/08-opa-1148.html. For an example of news coverage, see Brian C. Kalt, "Once Pardoned, Always Pardoned," *Washington Post,* January 25, 2009.

53. Office of the Press Secretary, "Statement by the Press Secretary," White House, December 24, 2008, https://www.presidency.ucsb.edu/documents/statement-the-press-secretary-1.

54. Kalt, "Once Pardoned, Always Pardoned."

55. See Aimee Picchi, "What Is an Autopen? Here's What to Know about the Device Used by Presidents, Writers, and More," *CBS News,* June 5, 2025, https://www.cbsnews.com/news/what-is-an-autopen-president-biden-trump-signature/.

56. "Whether the President May Sign a Bill by Directing That His Signature Be Affixed to It," Op. O.L.C., Vol. 29: (2005), 97.

57. Donald Trump (@realDonaldTrump), *Truth Social,* March 17, 2025 (edited June 26, 2025, 208:33 ETPM), https://truthsocial.com/@realDonaldTrump/posts/114175908922736427.

58. See Picchi, "What Is an Autopen?" (noting President Trump's remarks to reporters on Air Force that he used an autopen "only for very unimportant papers").

59. See also David Pozen, "The Deceptively Clear Twenty-Fifth Amendment," National Constitution Center, https://constitutioncenter.org/the-constitution/amendments/amendment-xxv/interpretations/159#the-deceptively-clear-twenty-fifth-amendment-by-david-pozen.

60. Trump White House, "Reviewing Certain Presidential Actions," June 14, 2025, https://www.whitehouse.gov/presidential-actions/2025/06/reviewing-certain-presidential-actions/.

61. US Const. amend. XXV, § 4.

62. Lee's proclamation is quoted in Alexander Hamilton to William Rawle, November 17–19 1794, in *The Papers of Alexander Hamilton,* vol. 17, ed. Harold C. Syrett (New York: Columbia University Press, 1972), 380n14; Hamilton cites *The [New York] Daily Advertiser,* December 6, 1794.

63. Charlie Savage and Tyler Pager, "Biden Says He Made the Clemency Decisions That Were Recorded with Autopen," *New York Times*, July 13, 2025.

64. Charlie Savage and Tyler Pager, "Biden Says He Made the Clemency Decisions."

65. James T. Wooten, "Legionnaires Boo Carter on Pardon for Draft Defiers," *New York Times*, August 25, 1976.

66. Angelo Fichera, "How Has Biden Done on His 2020 Campaign Promises?" *New York Times*, November 8, 2023.

67. Fichera, "How Has Biden Done?"

68. Alana Wise, "Biden's Pot Pardon Will Help Reverse War on Drugs Harm to Black People, Advocates Say," *NPR*, October 10, 2022, https://www.npr.org/2022/10/10/1127708285/marijuana-pardon-biden-black-people-war-on-drugs-harm.

69. Donald Trump (@realDonaldTrump), *Truth Social*, March 11, 2024 (edited June 26, 2025), https://truthsocial.com/@realDonaldTrump/posts/112079753989223875. To be fair to Donald Trump, sometimes he added qualifiers, as in this post's wording that he would pardon the "wrongfully" imprisoned. Various aides said it would be a case-by-case matter of pardoning the innocent. Even so, because he repeatedly described those convicted of January 6 crimes as "hostages" and "unbelievable patriots," it is fair to assume that many of them thought he was making a promise. And, of course, he did end up pardoning all of them.

70. Kevin Liptak, "Biden Pardons All Federal Offenses of Simple Marijuana Possession in First Major Steps Towards Decriminalization," *CNN*, October 6, 2022, https://www.cnn.com/2022/10/06/politics/marijuana-decriminalization-white-house-joe-biden; Angelo Fichera, "How Has Biden Done on His 2020 Campaign Promises?"

71. Biden White House, "Background Press Call on Marijuana Reform," press briefing, October 6, 2022, https://bidenwhitehouse.archives.gov/briefing-room/press-briefings/2022/10/06/background-press-call-on-marijuana-reform/.

72. Joseph R. Biden Jr., "A Proclamation on Granting Pardon for Offense of Simple Possession of Marijuana, Attempted Simple Possession of Marijuana, or Use of Marijuana," December 22, 2023, https://bidenwhitehouse.archives.gov/briefing-room/presidential-actions/2023/12/22/a-proclamation-on-granting-pardon-for-the-offense-of-simple-possession-of-marijuana-attempted-simple-possession-of-marijuana-or-use-of-marijuana/.

73. Joseph R. Biden Jr., "Statement from President Biden on Marijuana Reform," October 6, 2022, https://bidenwhitehouse.archives.gov/briefing-room/statements-releases/2022/10/06/statement-from-president-biden-on-marijuana-reform/.

74. Biden White House, "Background Press Call on Marijuana Reform."

75. Biden White House, "Background Press Call on Marijuana Reform."

76. To be clear, the pardon extended only to citizens and green card holders; it left in place the sanctions that might be imposed on people outside those groups. This was a policy pardon, but only for citizens and green card holders.

77. "Fact Sheet: President Biden Commutes the Sentences of 37 Individuals on Death Row," White House, December 12, 2024, https://bidenwhitehouse.archives .gov/briefing-room/statements-releases/2024/12/23/fact-sheet-president-biden -commutes-the-sentences-of-37-individuals-on-death-row/.

78. President Jimmy Carter, "Address to the American Legion Convention in Seattle, Washington," August 24, 1976, American Presidency Project, ed. Gerhard Peters and John T. Woolley, University of California, Santa Barbara, https://www .presidency.ucsb.edu/documents/address-the-american-legion-convention-seattle -washington.

79. English Bill of Rights 1689: "An Act Declaring the Rights and Liberties of the Subject and Settling the Succession of the Crown," The Avalon Project, Yale Law School Lillian Goldman Law Library, https://avalon.law.yale.edu/17th _century/england.asp.

80. U.S. Const. art. II, § 1, cl. 1.

81. "Relatives and Residents: Emilie (Emily) Todd Helm," Mr. Lincoln's White House, Lehrman Institute, https://www.mrlincolnswhitehouse.org/residents-visitors /relatives-and-residents/relatives-residents-emilie-emily-todd-helm/index.html.

82. Harold Holzer, ed., *The Lincoln Mailbag: America Writes to the President, 1861–1865* (Carbondale: Southern Illinois University Press, 1998), 117–118.

83. Ben Brasch, "Meet Roger Clinton, A First-Family Member Pardoned Long Before Hunter Biden," *Washington Post*, December 4, 2024.

84. Amy Goldstein, "House Report Faults Roger Clinton's Role in Pardons," *Washington Post*, March 13, 2002.

85. *United States v. Kushner*, No. 2:04-CR-00580 (DNJ 2004).

86. Jill Colvin and Colleen Long, "Kushner Pardon Revives 'Loathsome' Tale of Tax Evasion, Sex," AP, December 23, 2020, https://apnews.com/article/donald-trump -charles-kushner-new-jersey-elections-crime-0155d15fa31108fd2c0e6360a3b597dd.

87. Colvin and Long, "Kushner Pardon."

88. Joseph R. Biden, Jr., "Executive Grant of Clemency, Robert Hunter Biden," December 1, 2024, https://www.justice.gov/d9/2024-12/biden_warrant.pdf.

89. Joseph R. Biden, Jr., "Executive Grant of Clemency, James B. Biden, Sara Jones Biden, Valerie Biden Owens, John T. Owens, and Francis W. Biden," January 19, 2025, https://www.justice.gov/pardon/media/1385756/dl?inline.

90. Biden, Jr., "Executive Grant of Clemency, James B. Biden, Sara Jones Biden, Valerie Biden Owens, John T. Owens, and Francis W. Biden."

91. Brian C. Kalt, "Pardon Me? The Constitutional Case Against Presidential Self-Pardons," *Yale Law Journal* 106, no. 3 (1996): 779–809, 779–780.

92. Kalt, "Pardon Me?" 779.

93. "Presidential or Legislative Pardon of a President," Office of Legal Counsel (OLC) memo, 1 Op. O.L.C. Supp. 370, 370 (1974).

94. "Presidential or Legislative Pardon of a President," 371.

95. Kalt, "Pardon Me?" 779.

96. Meilan Solly, "When President Ulysses S. Grant Was Arrested for Speeding in a Horse-Drawn Carriage," *Smithsonian Magazine,* March 31, 2023.

97. *Trump v. United States,* 603 US 593, 609, 614–616 (2024).

98. US Const. art. II, § 2, cl. 1.

99. Kalt, "Pardon Me?" 806.

100. See, for example, *Burnham v. Superior Court,* 495 U.S. 604 (1990).

101. *United States v. Juror No. 1,* 866 F.Supp.2d 442, 447–49 (2011).

102. 2 U.S.C. § 4501.

103. 2 U.S.C. § 4701 et seq.

104. Act of March 2, 1853, § 2, 10 Stat. 172, 173.

105. Sherburne F. Cooke Jr., "The Little Napoleon: The Short and Turbulent Career of Isaac I. Stevens," *Columbia Magazine* 14, no. 4 (2000): 17–20, 17, https://www.washingtonhistory.org/wp-content/uploads/2020/04/little-napolean.pdf.

106. US Const. art I, § 9 cl. 2.

107. Cooke, "The Little Napoleon."

108. Isaac I. Stevens and Isaac M. Smith, "Governor Stevens' Famous Pardon of Himself, July 10, 1856," in *Washington Historical Quarterly* 25, no. 3 (1934): 229–230.

109. Cooke, "The Little Napoleon."

110. US Const. Art. II, § 3

111. US Const. Art. II, § 1

112. But see *United States v. Sanders,* 133 F. 4th 341, 395 (5th Cir. 2025) (Oldham, J., concurring) (criticizing President Biden's commutation of the death sentence handed down to a convicted kidnapper and murderer of a twelve-year-old child).

Chapter 7 · The Future of Twenty Words

1. Abraham Lincoln, "A House Divided," speech at Springfield, Illinois, June 16, 1858, in *Collected Works of Abraham Lincoln,* vol. 2, ed. Roy P. Basler (New Brunswick, NJ: Rutgers University Press, 1953), 461 (emphasis omitted).

2. Erica Bryant, "Presidents and Governors Should Pardon More People in Prison," Vera Institute of Justice, January 15, 2025, https://www.vera.org/news/presidents-and-governors-should-pardon-more-people-in-prison.

3. *United States v. Klein,* 80 US (13 Wall.) 128, 148 (1871) (Congress cannot limit or change the effect of a presidential pardon).

4. *Trump v. U.S.*, 603 U.S. 593, 608 (2024) (quoting *Klein*, 80 U.S. (13 Wall.), 143–144, 147–148; and then quoting *Youngstown Sheet & Tube Co. v. Sawyer*, 343 U.S. 579, 637–38 (1952) (Jackson, J., concurring)).

5. US Const. art. V.

6. Alexander Hamilton to William Rawle, November 17–19, 1794, *The Papers of Alexander Hamilton*, vol. 17, ed. Harold C. Syrett (New York: Columbia University Press, 1969), 380n14 (quoting *The Daily Advertiser*, December 6, 1794).

7. Graham G. Dodds, ed., *Mass Pardons in America: Rebellion, Presidential Amnesty, and Reconciliation* (New York: Columbia University Press, 2021), 192 (list three instances), 101 (Utah Territorial Governor Alfred Cumming pardoning additional offenses in Utah after James Buchanan had pardoned sedition and treason), 125 (describing Governor Andrew Johnson's pardon policy in Tennessee), 211 (Lincoln being told he could not delegate the power).

8. King George III, "The King's Speech upon Opening the Session, October 26, 1775," in *The Parliamentary History of England*, vol. 18, ed. T. C. Hansard (London: Hansard, 1813): 695–697, 697 (declaring that he would give authority to persons "upon the spot to grant general or particular pardons . . . as they shall think fit").

9. William F. Duker, "The President's Power to Pardon: A Constitutional History," *William and Mary Law Review* 18, no. 3 (1977): 475–538, 497–500.

10. See, for example, President Jimmy Carter, "Granting Pardon for Violations of the Selective Service Act, August 4, 1964 to March 28, 1973," Proclamation No. 4483, 91 Stat. 1719, January 21, 1977, https://www.govinfo.gov/content/pkg /STATUTE-91/pdf/STATUTE-91-Pg1719.pdf.

11. Donald J. Trump, "Granting Pardons and Commutation of Sentences for Certain Offenses Relating to the Events at or Near the United States Capitol on January 6, 2021," January 20, 2025, Proclamation No. 10887, 90 Fed. Reg. 8331, https://www.federalregister.gov/documents/2025/01/29/2025-01950/granting -pardons-and-commutation-of-sentences-for-certain-offenses-relating-to-the -events-at-or-near; Joseph R. Biden, "Granting Pardon for the Offense of Simple Possession of Marijuana," October 6, 2022, Proclamation 10467, 87 Fed. Reg. 61441, https://www.federalregister.gov/documents/2022/10/12/2022-22262/granting -pardon-for-the-offense-of-simple-possession-of-marijuana.

12. Donald J. Trump, "Granting Pardons and Commutation of Sentences for Certain Offenses Relating to the Events at or Near the United States Capitol on January 6, 2021," January 20, 2025, Proclamation No. 10887, 90 Fed. Reg. 8331.

13. See, for example, Act of May 26, 1790, ch. 12, 1 Stat. 122, 123 (granting power to remit to the treasury secretary); Act of March 3, 1791, ch. 15, 1 Stat. 199, 209; Act of March 3, 1797, ch. 13, 1 Stat. 506; Act of February 11, 1800, ch. 6, 2 Stat. 7 (renewing Act of March 3, 1797).

14. *Pollock v. Bridgeport Steam-Boat Co. (The Laura)*, 114 U.S. 411, 413–416 (1885).

15. Act of March 2, 1799, ch. 24, 1 Stat. 709, 714 (commander-in-chief of fleet can pardon any death sentence); Act of April 23, 1800, ch. 33, 2 Stat. 45, 51 (giving commander of fleet or squadron the power to pardon when a court martial trial occurred outside the United States).

16. Act of June 25, 1910, ch. 387, 44 Stat. 819.

Acknowledgments

I OWE DEBTS TO MANY. I wrote about presidential pardons before, in *Imperial from the Beginning* (New Haven: Yale University Press, 2015), a work that informs this one. Because pardons are in the news, for all the wrong reasons, it seemed worth reflecting upon facets of the pardon power in greater depth.

Thanks to my editor, Sharmila Sen, who drummed up the idea behind this book. Without her "Eureka" moment, this would not have come to pass. She expertly shepherded me through the whole process. Thanks also to her colleagues at Harvard University Press: Sam Mateo, Julia Kirby, and all the others who assisted behind the scenes.

Over the decades, I've discussed pardons with Larry Alexander, Jack Goldsmith, John Harrison, Mike Ramsey, Mike Rappaport, Steve Smith, and Cass Sunstein. I have learned much from each of these dear friends. I'm particularly grateful to Jack and Cass as they read an entire draft and supplied invaluable feedback and pushback.

I am extremely indebted to my terrific research assistants, stretching back to my time at the University of San Diego and through the present at the University of Virginia: Bradley J. Berklich, Anastasia Forbes, Olivia Haimerl, Tyler Hazen, Frederick (Trey) Kieser, Lance Ledet, Aleksander Mehta, Kawit Promrat, Suraj Renganathan, Kanishk Singh, and Milan Singh. Relatedly, I thank the superb law librarians at the University of Virginia for all their sleuthing on my behalf.

Finally, thanks to the University of Virginia for summer support, particularly my dean, Leslie Kendrick. That support allows me to work throughout the summer. In fact, I always ask myself, "Where would I be without summer research support?"

Invariably, the answer is the same: "The beach."

Index

·